REGENERATE

REGENERATE

FOLLOWING JESUS
AFTER DECONSTRUCTION

TONY SCARCELLO
foreword by KURT WILLEMS

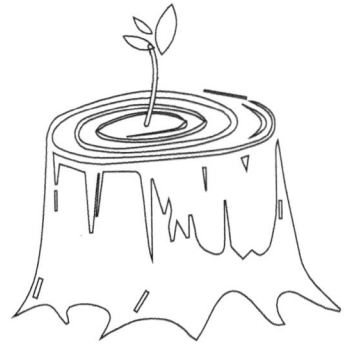

WIPF & STOCK · Eugene, Oregon

REGENERATE

Following Jesus after Deconstruction

Copyright © 2020 Tony Scarcello. All rights reserved. Except for brief quotations in critical publications or reviews, no part of this book may be reproduced in any manner without prior written permission from the publisher. Write: Permissions, Wipf and Stock Publishers, 199 W. 8th Ave., Suite 3, Eugene, OR 97401.

Wipf & Stock
An Imprint of Wipf and Stock Publishers
199 W. 8th Ave., Suite 3
Eugene, OR 97401

www.wipfandstock.com

PAPERBACK ISBN: 978-1-5326-8513-2
HARDCOVER ISBN: 978-1-5326-8514-9
EBOOK ISBN: 978-1-5326-8515-6

Manufactured in the U.S.A.

Dedicated to . . .

Kim Scarcello, David Lanning, and Wayne Dinnel. Knowing you are in the great cloud of witnesses is as good of motivation as I can imagine to run my race well.

And, Kelsey Scarcello. Thank you for running by my side through every peak and valley. With you in my life I get to experience the Good Life every day.

Contents

Foreword by Kurt Willems | ix
Introduction | 1

Part I Beautiful Faith Shackled in Shame

1. The Wonderful and Terrible Trend of Deconstruction | 7
2. Conservative Saints and Tongues of Fire | 18
3. Locked in Secret | 28
4. Nothing Stands between Us | 37
5. Church | 47
6. Remember You Like Yesterday | 55
7. The Twists in My Story | 58
8. Slippery Slope | 67
9. There I Find You in the Mystery | 81

Part II A Faith Worth Passing Down

10. The Donkey, the Elephant, and the Lamb | 95
11. The Jesus of Suburbia is a Lie | 116
12. What is a Healthy Construct? | 127
13. Regenerate | 141
14. Acknowledgments | 149

Bibliography | 153

Foreword

DECONSTRUCTION IS A WORD with many meanings. For some Christians it is a buzz word for "safe." For others, "heresy." And still for others, a word before a better word, "reconstruction"—or in the case of my friend Tony Scarcello, *Regenerate*.

In the last two decades, the word "deconstruction" has left the ivory towers of philosophy and has given language to those of us who wrestle with wanting to follow Jesus without the cultural boxes he's been contained in. Choices made about theology, even a generation or two prior, easily make their way into pockets of Christian culture as though things have "always been this way." Then, something happens…

- A family member dies.
- A marriage ends.
- A friend comes out of the closet.
- A science class teaches, well, science.
- A non-Christian demonstrates Christlike love.
- A video leaks about unarmed Black men being killed by police (and another, then another, and another after that).
- A war no longer feels like a Godly cause.
- A Christian friend betrays you.
- A church silences your questions.
- A non-Christian friend dies.

FOREWORD

A woman preaches the Bible and inspires you when such was called sinful in your home church.

A pandemic kills lots of people and Christians fight about it.

A political ideology no longer feels sanctified.

A silence from God . . .

And this list is the mere tip of the faith-crisis iceberg.

People walk away from faith in Jesus all the time for these and various other reasons. Some experiences raise questions that transcend the space allotted for exploration within many Christian communities. The sad truth is this: *The church does a fine job at creating atheists.*

What do I mean? Without gracious space for people to be vulnerable, to truly be honest about the mess and struggle in their lives, many eventually walk away from God. There is a broad Christian community—especially in but not limited to the USA—that passes down prepackaged "right answers." And look, I'm not saying Christianity isn't rooted in clear essential beliefs: God created the universe, God is triune, Jesus' death saves us from evil, Jesus literally rose from the dead, the Spirit abides with us, Jesus will return, etc.

I'm saying those essentials are constantly heaped with baggage that silences questions with absolutes rather than stepping into the doubts and pain of people with holy curiosity. If we truly trust the Spirit to speak, what's the risk of curiosity in the context of community? I think it's less risky than creating systems of dogma that force-feeds doses of shame until (especially) young adults decide to go on a spiritual hunger strike, sometimes permanently.

Rather than creating space to explore ideas, to stare in the face each question that arises from "the things that happen," Christian culture sometimes upends its mission to make disciples. Someone might have a crisis of creation: "Genesis says seven days so don't ask me about *evil*-lution!" Or a crisis of their picture of God: "God the Father beat up Jesus to show us love." Or a crisis of political allegiances: "To be a true Christian you must vote like this." Each faith-crisis, when confronted with clichés, leaves many people to decide if they are going to accept the whole package or nothing at all. The problem is, as many of us have found out, the gift of Jesus is often so covered by the wrappings of religiosity that some no longer access what they've boxed up: the uncontainable love of God. American Christians: we've got a problem. Truth be told, collectively, we've caused it. But it doesn't have to be this way. We can create disciples without creating atheists.

It's no surprise, then, why we *need* books like *Regenerate: Following Jesus after Deconstruction*. My friend Tony authentically unwraps his life as a gift for his readers. He brings us into the pain of keeping part of his story under wraps for most of his life. Tony is honest about the trauma and struggles with his family. He gives us a heartbreaking story of feeling rejected by so many in the church who claimed to love him. And here's the thing about Tony: he does all of this without any hint of snark or bitterness. The reason Tony can do this is because although he almost let go of faith altogether for a season, he discovered a God who refuses to let go of him.

Here's the thing about Tony Scarcello that you need to know: he deconstructed his beliefs which gave the Holy Spirit the space to partner with him in reconstructing his heart. We might even say Jesus invited him to *regenerate* his faith in continuity with the past, and with a sense of freedom and joy for the present. Some may hear words like "deconstruction" and think, *So he finally figured out the Bible isn't authoritative.* Or, *He finally decided all paths lead to being "spiritual."* Nope. This journey led Tony to the Jesus depicted in the New Testament: the radical question-asker, the eternally curious one, the partier with sinners, the nonviolent revolutionary, the full expression of who God *has* been and *will* always be: incomprehensible, others-oriented, love. Tony has found more Jesus, not less.

So, I invite you to step into Tony's story. And I'm going to be honest, you might tear up a few times. *I'm not crying, you're crying!* His story is raw, but wow, it's so full of hope. Tony shows us God never stops pursuing, never stops loving, and never stops seeking to redeem our pain. In *Regenerate*, you not only get Tony's tragically hope-filled story, but you're invited to encounter the gift of the Jesus he's discovered under the wrappings of legalism and shame. Tony isn't only an example of someone following Jesus after deconstruction, but shows us God is gently calling each of us to be regenerated through our pain, doubts, and questions. I'm so grateful he wrote this book and couldn't be more excited for you to read it too! Maybe, if more people in Christian churches engage with a resource like this, the need for intense deconstruction will itself deconstruct as the people of God create a new kind of Jesus-shaped church culture.

Kurt Willems (July 2020) ||| pastor, podcaster (TheologyCurator.com), and author of *Echoing Hope: How the Humanity of Jesus Redeems our Pain* (forthcoming, March 2021)

Introduction

IN THE GOSPEL OF John chapter eighteen, we catch the great apostle Peter in his most shameful moment. Peter stands around a charcoal fire with a group of onlookers as Christ is being interrogated. One of the onlookers recognizes Peter as an associate of Jesus. Three times Peter denies knowing Jesus, and just as the Son of Man foretold, the caw of a rooster rings in the disciple's ears, forcing him to lock eyes with Jesus. Jesus—the best friend Peter ever had, his rabbi, the one who revealed his true identity, and released him into an adventure full of miracles, love, and fulfillment. Peter looked him in the eyes and I imagine began to weep as he ran away.

Three chapters later Jesus watches Peter from afar next to a charcoal fire. But rather than reject or deny the disciple, Jesus makes him breakfast, a sign in the ancient world that one considers the other family. And to subvert history even more, Jesus brings Peter into a circumstance where he again has to repeat something three times; but rather than the statements being words of denial, the statements are words of love. The biblical author intentionally uses imagery from the moment of Peter's failure and Jesus asks Peter to reaffirm his love for him three times for a reason—Jesus knows that only by confronting his past can Peter be equipped to step into his future.

> Jesus knows that only by confronting his past can Peter be equipped to step into his future.

It was after Peter's greatest failure that he would lead the Jesus movement, not before. It was after the failure that Peter would preach a sermon during Pentecost that brought thousands into the movement, not before. Peter failed, and it was not the end of his story. But after the failure, and

INTRODUCTION

before stepping into God's preferred future, Peter had to walk with Jesus through the confrontation of his past.

This book is my process of walking with Christ to confront my past. It is a work years in the making, birthed from a constellation of beauty and pain, hope and despair, failure and triumph. I started writing this story in 2016 as I was grieving the death of a dream. But the idea to turn it into a book was given to me by a dear friend shortly after it was made clear to me God was not done with my dreams. I wrote this to have a space where I could confront the collective experiences that made me who I am. I also write it because I know my experience is not an isolated one. I write this as a pastor, a pastor who has undergone an arduous and lengthy season of doubt in God, anger at the church, and fear I would never again be able to honestly call myself a Christian.

My hope with this book is to provide an analysis of the crises of faith many in my generation are experiencing in this cultural moment. This is not a work of academia—this is my story. The best analysis I can provide is data collected from my own experience and the experiences of the ones around me. My hope is that this work will be a resource to the beloved community of God, for those who worship with utter certainty in their doctrines and beliefs, and for those who feel like they are on the edge of the inside of Christianity, those who fear they are on their way out. There is a rising number of people in the church today who are plagued by doubt and hurt, feeling as though they are on their way out. This book is for you, and this book is for people who love you.

But this book is not just my story. The book is in two parts: the first accounts for my process of construction, deconstruction, and reconstruction. Deconstruction is a phenomenon taking place in many who once considered themselves devout to a faith, belief, or idea. It is a process of spiritual violence, pain, and often times trauma. Some degree of deconstruction is inevitable—theology and practice will take on new shapes and forms as each generation inherits the faith. Yet I question the wisdom in glamorizing such a process. The second part of this book is a discourse of ways we can address certain things in the church that are causing the unnecessary crises of faith many are experiencing.

Before we proceed, I do want to discuss some terms. A defining factor in my story has been the process of sorting through my sexual identity. As a man who experiences same-sex attraction, I tell this story at great risk to myself, my wife, family, friends, and church. With a topic this heated and

INTRODUCTION

important as this, there is no way to have the discussion without raising eyebrows and inviting scrutiny. I have attempted to handle the issue with as much sensitivity and nuance as possible. With as hotly debated as the topic is, I must express in no uncertain terms that my story is not up for debate. If you need this topic handled with specific language and titles, know now that I have not acquiesced to this impulse. My story is one of a man who has struggled through a nearly lifelong experience of same-sex attraction, and who is happily married to the girl of his dreams. I know this does not fit the narrative certain political and theological groups have tried to shape for the public, but I am thrilled by my decision to remain faithful to my convictions, and stay married to the girl of my dreams. I am presenting my wholehearted self.

The other thing I must address from the get-go is how I use the word "church." I address "the church" many times in this book, and I almost always mean it as a reference to the American church as a whole. I am not throwing one or two specific churches under the bus; I am speaking of the broader collective of Christians in my country. My hope in this book is not to dishonor anyone who has been a part of my spiritual journey; I hope to take responsibility for my own zeal while also uncomplicatedly pointing things out that must change should we wish for the incoming generations to take up the mantle of faith.

I want to forewarn readers that I present the specific things which tripped me up in my faith journey without pulling punches. I do not do this to glamorize the process or lure people into a similar experience. I opted for brutal honesty because I hope this book finds its way to a reader who is wrestling their way through similar cognitive dissonances. You may read about things I struggled with and it may cause some stress on your part; however, keep reading. I hope to address the specific things which tripped me up. My desire is not to create a crisis of faith, but to ease the pain of those experiencing one, or help the loved ones of those experiencing one.

May this book serve as an invitation to a deepened connectivity in the church, not a cause for division. I am grieving the recent loss of a dear friend, mentor, boss, pastor, and spiritual father. His name was David Lanning, and he made the decision to invest in me well before I was ready to rejoin the ministry. He saw the ways in which he and I thought differently, read the Bible differently, practiced certain aspects of faith differently, and he leaned in. "*Who you are is more important to me than what you do,*" he would tell me on an almost weekly basis in the few years I spent working for

INTRODUCTION

him. Pastor Dave and I shared sacred space together, space where we did not always see eye to eye, but we always connected heart to heart. It wasn't until his passing earlier this year that I realized our relationship modeled for me what I hope to see in the broader church.

Lastly, may this book serve as a companion to those who journey the painful road of faith, disenchantment with religion, and determination to hang on to Christ in spite of it all. If you are reading this and you have not undergone the philosophical upheaval of deconstruction yourself, may this work serve as a guide to you as you attempt to serve the inevitable loved ones you will meet in church who do suffer the journey. We are the church, and we are in this thing together.

Grace and peace.

Part I

Beautiful Faith Shackled in Shame

CHAPTER ONE

The Wonderful and Terrible Trend of Deconstruction

"My idea of God is not a Divine idea. It has to be shattered from time to time. He shatters it himself. He is the great iconoclast."
—C.S. LEWIS

"I cry out, 'my splendor is gone! Everything I had hoped for from the LORD is lost!'"
—LAMENTATIONS 3:18 (NLT)

He Deserved Better

IT'S EARLY SPRING OF 2016 and I'm sitting in the hospital room of a fifteen-year-old boy who has just slit his wrists. For the sake of confidentiality, we'll call him Jack. I work at a halfway house for teenage boys in Eugene, Oregon. At this point in my life, I am mentoring and counseling students who have served their sentence in a juvenile detention center but are behaviorally and psychologically unprepared to be transitioned into society. Sometimes we get to look after them for a few months; other times we have them for over a year. Yes, they are all guilty of crimes, but everyone has a context. Every one of these kids has a story tragic enough to make the average person shudder. Jack's particularly tugged at my heart. He is kind, compassionate, and devoted to his process—but he didn't attempt to take his life for no reason.

PART I: BEAUTIFUL FAITH SHACKLED IN SHAME

He was born in Astoria, Oregon, and lived with his mom, dad, and older brother. When he turned seven, his father brought him along to the factory where he worked. He took him to the janitor's closet and said to his child: "Son, your mom and I don't have a lot of money. Today, you get to be a man and help take care of the family." Jack recalls his father saying this with tears in his eyes. He had never seen his father cry before. His dad's co-workers would then pay to spend time with Jack in the closet, taking turns raping and molesting him. Every Thursday, for years, Jack would go to work with his dad, be locked in a closet, and be horrifically abused by older men with a history of pedophilia. Eventually Jack finally told his aunt and uncle what had been taking place. His father was immediately arrested. Without a steady source of income, his mother turned to dealing heroin, even giving some to her kids to "calm them down" on their more rowdy days; and consequently, by the time he was twelve, Jack was a full-blown addict. Soon, his mother would go jail, resulting in Jack bouncing from foster home to foster home. Some home environments were just as abusive and destructive as the closet at the factory; others were brief glimpses of kindness and love.

By the time he started going through puberty Jack had been conditioned to view sex as a nonconsensual expression of dominance, and Jack would then subject his foster siblings to the same abuse he had endured. After getting caught, Jack ran away from home. When he was fourteen years old the police found him overdosed on a park bench. He was sentenced to juvenile detention. A little over a year later, he was sent to the halfway house where I worked.

Jack and I formed a bond as soon as we met. We had similar interests, a similar sense of humor, and we both had a desire for him to do well in life. By the time I met him, he seemed to be doing really well. He was getting good grades, he was doing the difficult work of counseling, processing, and setting up personal boundaries to make himself a safe and sustainable person. For the first time in his life, he had plans for life after high school: go to college, study business, and open up a skate shop. I believed he could do it, but more importantly, so did he.

This night was different, though. Jack received a visit from his brother, who explained to him his father had hung himself in prison.

After his brother left, Jack locked himself in the bathroom, broke the mirror, and cut his wrists.

He rationalized to himself that he was responsible for his father's death: if he had said nothing about the abuse, maybe his dad would not have been sent to jail, and maybe he would still be alive.

So here I sit in this hospital room with him and my supervisor. Jack is asleep, his arms sown back up and wrapped in bandages. I sit by his bed, with his blood still on my shirt, my head bowed, and I try to pray.

I try to pray, but I can't.

All I can think about is, *What if he succeeded? What if he slit his wrists and then he died? And that's his life, his story. He is born, has seven supposedly decent years, then eight years of rape, torture, addiction, and shame; and then suicide. And after all of that? A final destination to hell, where he would suffer forever.*

Because you see, this kid had not yet prayed what we called in my circles "The Sinner's Prayer." Jack didn't believe in God. And my personal faith system up to this point has always asserted you must confess with your mouth that Jesus is Lord and believe in your heart that God raised him from the dead, or you could not be saved. Saved from what? From the wrath of a God who needed to punish the sin done against him and his creation, who would lock us in the eternal conscious torment of hell. I believed it was only by God's grace and my ability to recognize Christ's atoning work on the cross I wouldn't suffer the same fate. My theology dictates Jack had to go to hell forever if he died because he sinned and had not repented.

Some might say, "Well thank God, he didn't succeed in killing himself." And I agree! Thank God. Jack survived and would go back to the halfway house, and graduate the program. Thank God he would go on to live with a rehabilitated mom and graduate high school.

But here is one thought I cannot shake: *there are a lot of kids with stories similar to his, and there are a lot of kids who don't believe in God (or they believe in the wrong god) and they do succeed in taking their own lives.*

What about them?

Are they in hell? Are they burning forever?

Barring substantial miraculous intervention, I could not imagine believing in a God of love and justice if I had gone through what Jack went through. Who could blame him for his atheism?

As I sat in the hospital room, a conversation I had with this kid a few weeks prior came to mind. He was browsing the internet (as I monitored him) and came across an article that read something along the lines of: "Megachurch Pastor Thanks God for His Ten-Million-Dollar House!" Jack,

PART I: BEAUTIFUL FAITH SHACKLED IN SHAME

who knew I used to be a youth pastor, looked at me and asked: "Why does God give that guy a ten-million-dollar house, but I can't get him to bail me out just a little bit?"

The question stung. I knew this was a loaded inquiry, and I wanted to choose my words carefully.

I replied, "I don't think God gave him that house. I think he's just saying that so he can show it off and not feel guilty about the amount of people's tithe money he spent on it."

Jack chuckled at my judgmental comment and moved on to another article. Still, I knew I had not adequately answered the real question he was asking. Why does God answer some prayers—like prayers for a promotion, a new house, or a new car—and ignore other prayers like, "Please rescue me from the gross men at Daddy's work?"

Jack wasn't stupid. He asked the right questions.

Again, I ask, who could blame him for his atheism?

I'm in the hospital room and the anger within me grows at the thought of kids with stories like these going to hell. That's the best infrastructure the Creator of the universe could design? The God of love? The God of hope, peace, justice—this is the best he could do? Jack didn't ask to exist—none of us did. What right does God have to will us into existence only to thrust us into hell because of a sin-condition we never asked for? All of a sudden, I feel like I could come up with a much better design for humanity. Hubris? Of course. Honest? Absolutely. It is one of the most honest moments I ever had with God.

I try to bypass those questions and just focus on connecting with the Spirit. I try to pray for Jack. I try to pray for my doubts. When that doesn't work I try to ignore them and press in to trust the Father—but there is one big problem:

None of this makes sense anymore. And it hasn't made sense to me for some time.

Deconstructing Deconstruction

I am far from the first person to experience an existential crisis because of human suffering, especially when that suffering falls on innocent children. This is a conundrum people have been wrestling with for thousands of years. There's even a fancy word for the problem—theodicy. A theodicy is a theological construct which attempts to vindicate God's goodness in

THE WONDERFUL AND TERRIBLE TREND OF DECONSTRUCTION

the presence of evidential evil or suffering. This problem of evil has created countless atheists, agnostics, deists, and has haunted Christians from every denomination.

That moment in the hospital marked a quickening of a faith reevaluation that had been taking place in me for a while. There are a lot of names for this transition. Paul Ricoeur called it "the transition from the *first to second naiveté.*"[1] Brian Zahnd affectionately refers to it as a process of going from "water to wine."[2] The most popular term in philosophical circles right now is "deconstruction." The term was coined by Algerian-French philosopher Jacques Derrida.[3] Deconstruction is the critical analysis of one's belief system. You take apart different aspects of a belief, piece by piece, and analyze what is worth keeping and what needs to be discarded. I've heard deconstruction compared to the furniture and appliances in a house. Sometimes you take a couch (an idea in your belief system) out and replace it with another one. Sometimes you take a bunch of furniture out at once, and the room feels empty for a while. This marks a time of being unsure of the particulars of your faith. Or sometimes you will violently demolish the house all together, meaning there is no longer any faith in what was once there.

Deconstruction is becoming an increasingly common phenomenon among young evangelical Christians, spawning the ever growing *Exvangelical* movement. Before the movement, the trend was to just abandon your faith all together. There was no rearranging the furniture in your spiritual house, only demolition or leaving it alone. There was no space for an in-between that allowed time to figure things out. Thanks to work done by men and women who are often heralded as heretics by more conservative tribes (folks like Rob Bell, Brian McLaren, the late Rachel Held Evans, and The Liturgists podcast crew, to name a few), language is being put to this frustrating experience. And, to be totally fair, before my own deconstruction, I too would have called them heretics. Before I needed a space for the in-between, I saw no need for an in-between. I viewed advocates of the in-between as nothing more than false teachers tickling the ears of those searching for something more palatable but less true. And even if today I find myself often times disagreeing with some of the content put out by these folks, more and more people are being given space and tools to

---

1. Ricoeur, *Symbolism of Evil.*
2. Zahnd, *Water to Wine.*
3. Derrida, *Of Grammatology.*

deconstruct without having to throw everything away at once. That is not something to reject all together—that should be celebrated.

That evening with Jack, my faith had taken a heavy blow. Or, to put it more accurately, it was when I realized my faith had been taking heavy blows for a while. This was alarming, as it always is when you realize you built your house on sand. My faith was a Jenga tower: the wrong block had been pulled and it was finally falling apart. This was alarming for another reason, however: I was afraid because I had never been given the tools or the permission to doubt or question the theology I inherited. Doubt was considered spiritual rebellion to some of the people I spent time with, the books I read, and sermons I'd listened to.

> We were taught that people didn't doubt because there was anything wrong with our belief system or because there were unanswerable questions—they doubted because they wouldn't humble themselves before God.

Sure, we'd entertain questions and some doubts—so long as you acted satisfied with the platitudes you were fed in response to your inquiry. Questioning doctrine was akin to making God in your image rather than submitting to the process of being made in God's image (as if all of humanity didn't inherently carry the image of God). We shamed doubt and forced ourselves to allow cheap, hokum responses to be our answers to costly questions. We were taught that people didn't doubt because there was anything wrong with our belief system or because there were unanswerable questions—they doubted because they wouldn't humble themselves before a God whose "ways were higher than our ways, whose thoughts were better than our thoughts" (Isa 55:8–9 NKJV).

The preconceived notion here is that doctrine is completely true and need not be questioned. The people who taught me these things, and the people they learned them from, were good and trustworthy people. What reason would there be to call these things into question? You were expected to make the assumption that what you were being taught was pure, sure-fire truth. The particulars of the faith system were treated as gospel. To question one part was to question the whole thing. There was no room for mystery, doubt, concessions, or scrutiny. We were led to believe questioning the authority of doctrine was to question the authority of God. I never stopped to probe the construct I was handed to see if it was healthy, good, or sustainable. I jumped from accepting it to finding every way to defend it. I treated doctrine as if it were as divine as *the* Divine.

Deconstruction flies right in the face of this reasoning. It happens when you realize your belief system is not infallible, when what you've always believed in reveals itself to be a manmade construct. This deconstruction process takes place when you try to make a construct fit in a place it couldn't possibly fit. In my case, I was trying to reconcile my theology of God and the afterlife with the tension I was experiencing, and I was doing so with all the success of trying to fit a square peg in a round hole. My construct did not work anymore. I could not accept that God cared about love and justice *and* would be willing to send Jack to hell forever, especially after what he had been through. My options were disbelief in God all together, rejection of God all together, or take a second look at this God I thought I knew everything about. I attempted the road of reevaluation, but because I fundamentally believed in an all or nothing doctrine, this process started taking my faith apart. And I began to feel like I was totally unravelling.

I had friends who underwent the deconstruction process. I saw their Facebook posts and blogs and tried correcting what I considered to be their rebellion and hubris. I joined fellow Christians in lamenting the "slippery slope" these friends allowed themselves to travel. I resented the deconstruction process and avoided it as much as possible.

But it was happening to me. Soon, I realized I was deconstructing so much more than just my afterlife theology. My whole faith house was going down. After facing the death of my mom, loss of my calling, shame in my marriage, rejection in my relationships, loss of my community, a nasty political season (where my tribe at the time, evangelicals, were some of the most vicious assailants), and a brutal introduction to how deep in the dark humanity can go, everything was being called into question—not just being called into question, but violently scrutinized. I had had enough of the type of Christianity I had been living, but because I spent so much time vilifying Christians who practiced and believed anything different than I once did, I thought that also had to mean I had had enough of Jesus.

Enough of this

I later realized it was not Jesus I was rejecting; it was not even always historic Christianity (though sometimes it was). I was revolting against *a way of practicing Christianity* that felt narrow in intellectual scope, caustic to

PART I: BEAUTIFUL FAITH SHACKLED IN SHAME

alternative ideas, and hubristic in its hermeneutic. I was revolting against a way of practicing faith that was more concerned with American idealism than with the new humanity Paul talked about in Ephesians 2. My way of following Jesus was obsessed with defining who was "us" and who were "them." And once I figured that out, I worked hard to keep us separated from them. We were the Christians—everybody else got a different title. If you were gay, liberal, interpreted the Bible differently, smoked pot, got drunk, had premarital sex, or were Catholic, you were not one of us. No matter how much you may have insisted you were a Christian, I always thought to myself or asserted out loud that you, in fact, were not a Christian (and don't even get me started on the Eastern Orthodox). On my more generous days, I'd concede you were a carnal or lukewarm Christian. When it came to the big questions of creation, life, meaning, God, the devil, heaven, hell, sacred texts, and how to interpret said texts, nobody had it figured out better than me and the ones who taught me.

But now all of that was falling apart. I was revolting against my own self-righteous and arrogant way of living and thinking. Today I now realize the way of practicing faith I was revolting against was not historic Christianity—it was a very modern American evangelicalism, a tribe in which I was deeply saturated and in a lot of ways still am. The biggest problem in all of this is it was extremely difficult for me to remove Jesus from the context of American evangelicalism. So, I didn't just abandon the system—for a while I abandoned Jesus, too.

According to Pew Research Center, in 2014 roughly 70 percent of Americans identified as Christian, a staggering 8 percent drop from 2007,[4] and the numbers don't show any signs of these percentages going up. Vast amounts of people raised in the church leave it after they graduate, and at one point studies were saying eight out of ten people,[5] though those studies are being called into question. And while many inside the church claim total confusion over why so many leave, for those outside the church the answers seem obvious. There is a lot of baggage that comes with being a Christian in America today, baggage that Jesus never intended us to carry. To be a Christian in our country in this present day comes with a tough and heavy load, one that does not seem to reflect the light-and-easy burden promised to us by Jesus. The world is growing less and less patient with the judgmental, graceless, materialistic, and tribal tendencies of American

---

4. Pew Research Center, "America's Changing Religious Landscape,".
5. Ham, *Already Gone: Why your kids will quit church and what you can do to stop it*

evangelicalism. Much of those things need to be burned away in the Refiner's fire—but we cannot afford to lose Jesus in the process.

We need to let go of much of what American Christianity has taught us, because much of it is more American than it is Christian, but we also need to hang onto the precious center of reality itself—as revealed in the life, teachings, death, and resurrection of Jesus. This paradox of simultaneously letting go and hanging on must be engaged with. We must not lose Jesus while letting go of what is more American idealism than Christianity. Without hanging onto what is most precious about the tradition, we can lose Jesus. So, we must learn to live in the tension of hanging on and letting go because we cannot afford to lose Jesus. For all my doubt, questions, and frustrations with the church, if there is one thing I believe more than anything else, it is that this world needs Jesus.

The world needs the teachings of Jesus, teachings which condemn those who cling to their power and wealth, teachings that elevate the cause of the outcast and the oppressed. The world needs the stories of Jesus's life that illustrate the incarnation of the Creator as a vulnerable child who grew up and dined with the dirty and left-out, not the political and religious elite. The world needs the death and resurrection of Jesus, the precious hope that the most final and diabolical force on the planet—death itself—has been disarmed by resurrection life. The world needs the activity of Jesus, which, as Aaron Niequist says in *The Eternal Current*, is always flowing like a river that rushes toward the healing and restoration of all things. As my late mentor and spiritual father, Dave Lanning, used to say, the world needs an invitation to swim right in the center of God's goodness. The world needs the natural and supernatural implications of the God who came and lived the human life, because human life matters. All of human life. All the time. From womb to tomb.

Hear me when I say I am not shaming the deconstruction process. Sometimes it is a person's only option. It can also be an enlightening experience where the richness of mystery and the revelation of love make God seem bigger and better than you ever thought before. As Brian Zahnd says in his book *Water to Wine*, it can be a time of leaving the cheap and simple water for the rich and complex wine. So, let us focus on why it is we deconstruct at all. I don't think we deconstruct because of Jesus; we deconstruct because what we were given does not look enough like Jesus. I think if the construct we were given accurately reflected the Christ of the Scriptures and the cosmos most people would feel little need to tear it down. Because, to this day, for believers and unbelievers alike, whether you're talking about Christ as a literal historical figure or as a compelling religious allegory, Jesus is the most beautiful thing that has ever happened to humanity.

The fear I have is sometimes we deconstruct so much we lose Jesus along the way, which renders the painful and frustrating process of deconstruction a waste because we will end up much the same kind of person we were, just with different opinions.

At its best, deconstruction is a way we remove every idea, habit, doctrine, or attitude that prevents us from fully embracing the life of the crucified and resurrected God. The process can lead to tremendous growth and internal change, and it can lead others to do the same. It can bring enlightenment, inclusion, and love. It can be labor pains that give birth to a more Christlike expression of Christianity.

At its worst, deconstruction belittles the precious power of Jesus and his story to the point where it becomes nothing more than an exercise in intellectual assent, and there is no soul transformation in it, nor is there the call toward radical obedience to the world-healing teachings of the Messiah. We are every bit as judgmental, hubristic, self-destructive, and fundamentalist as we were before . . . we are just fighting on a different side. Worst of all, deconstruction gone wrong takes us out of the game.

What's the game?

I agree with Aaron Niequist when he says the activity of Jesus, or the kingdom of God, is like a river that flows toward restoration and redemption, and we are invited to swim at the center of that flow and not be content to drift to the side. We are invited to participate in this mission of healing and redeeming, and we become most effective at this when we seek to take on the yoke (a way of living, seeing, thinking, and reading Scripture) of Jesus as our own yoke.

Deconstruction at its best makes this possible. Deconstruction at its worst keeps this from happening. This is why deconstruction is both a beautiful and terrible trend.

I swam close to the edge. I almost demolished the house.

I am not here in an attempt to prevent people from calling their faith into question. In fact, there are a lot of people I wish would get on it already. If you have been handed a construct that does not accurately reflect the generous love of Christ, or if you have been handed a construct that tells you the personal choices you make don't matter to God, some level of deconstruction may be necessary for you. It was for me. But I want to see a Christianity passed down that does not require violent deconstruction in order to find a more beautiful gospel. Additionally, I want to encourage the idea that when we deconstruct, as we fall into mystery, when it feels there is nothing we can hang on to, we can cling to Jesus like our lives depend on it.

Some people who are in the trenches of deconstruction may want to know why it's so important to hang onto Jesus when it feels everything is being ripped away. We'll get to that. Others may want a deeper understanding as to why this process of faith-crisis takes place at all. To do that, I need look no further than my own story.

CHAPTER TWO

Conservative Saints and Tongues of Fire

"How did You come to me? In what shape, what disguise?"
—*THE TREE OF LIFE*, 2011

"How precious is your unfailing love, O God! All of humanity finds shelter in the shadow of your wings."
—PSALM 36:7 (NLT)

In the Beginning

TO UNDERSTAND WHY DECONSTRUCTION happened to me, I first must give you a picture of the construct I was handed. I'm told the following definitely happened...

I must have been four or five years old, and I just learned how to go to the bathroom all by myself, without parental supervision (something I'm still proud of). I have had some friends get excited about their natural bodily functions, but nobody could rival my level of enthusiasm over what I had accomplished on that toilet. It may have been my first exposure to pride. I ran out of the bathroom in my family's little two-bedroom duplex wearing nothing but what I'm sure was my prized Batman underwear, and I beckoned my father to come with me to the lavatory. Apparently, I've been searching for applause my whole life.

"Come see! Come see!" I demanded as I grabbed my dad by the hand and pulled him to the toilet. We approached the porcelain throne and beheld the image of a four-year-old's pride.

"Oh wow!" my dad exclaimed. "You made a Clinton!"

"Yup!" I said, with a proud grin on my face.

Now you may have been caught off guard by the word my father chose to attribute to my potty-training trophy, but I wasn't.

You see, this was 1996, and Bill Clinton was our president. And let's just say my dad has some strong opinions about the forty-second president of the United States—none of which are positive. In fact, I did not know the difference between the words "poop" and "Clinton" until I was six or seven years old.

This is my background, this was the world I was born in to: a world of conservative ideals formed by some amazing and hilarious parents.

I had a childhood most could only dream of. Two loving parents who were devoted to my brother and me and to each other. We were a family that took trips to Disneyland and Disneyworld, camping trips, trips to Washington to see family, and frequent day trips to the Oregon coast. We had a weekly family night: every Thursday evening my parents would blow up a queen-sized air mattress in the living room, my dad would pop a giant bowl of popcorn, and we would watch *Survivor* and *CSI*. The greatest gift I was given by my parents as a child was that they always seemed to enjoy having my brother and me around. They didn't tolerate our presence; they enjoyed our existence. Of course, things didn't stay this way forever, but my formative years were filled with a love that was protective and nurturing.

If there were two things my parents instilled in my brother and me as the two most crucial truths, it was the Christian faith (more specifically, the Pentecostal kind) and Republican ideology. We worshiped Jesus as Lord and held Ronald Reagan up as one of our saints.

It took me a while to figure out politics, but Jesus was easy to fall in love with right away. The earliest memory I have is of me hearing about this Jesus guy and wanting everything to do with him.

My First Love

I was four years old with my mom in her room. With my head rested on her lap she ran her fingers through my golden blonde hair. I practiced my impressions of dogs and cats, horses and elephants. This moment hangs in my memory like a picture on the walls of a hallway. She laughed and then said something to me that she would repeat for the rest of her life:

"Honey, I love you more than life itself."

Even as I write these words I'm filled with the warm sensation of being loved by my mom.

"But do you know who loves you even more than I do?"

I paused for a moment before responding, "Daddy?"

"Daddy loves you the same as me. Jesus. Jesus loves you more than anyone could ever love you."

I moved my eyes from my mother's and looked up at her white bedroom ceiling. I pondered how this could be. I heard my parents talk about Jesus and about him at church, but I don't think I heard it put like this before. Here was my mother, to me the source of love itself, claiming there is one who has a deeper love than even she had for me. At first I was grieved, thinking this somehow meant my mom loved me less. When I expressed my fret to her, she responded:

"Jesus loves you so much that he created you. You are alive because Jesus loves you. All of us can make good things with our love, but his love creates the most beautiful things. No matter how much I love you, my love would never be able to create something as beautiful as you. Only Jesus's love could do that."

In that moment, my mom taught me two things that were so theologically rich there is no way a four-year-old could understand it:

1. That I am an expression of Gods creative love.
2. Love creates. Every great piece of art, from Rembrandt's *The Prodigal Son* to Chance the Rapper's *Finish Line*, was birthed into existence as an expression of love. In a world that is filled to the brim with a hate that destroys so many people, Jesus stands as the image of creative love.

"Can I meet Jesus?" I asked of her.

My mom then told me I only needed to pray, and if I listen, sometimes he will talk back. She told me about sin and how we all do it. She told me about grace and how God has offered it to me. She told me about saying sorry for the things we've done wrong and that God will always forgive. Of course, I didn't understand much of what she was saying at the time; I think I barely understand it all now. But she got her point across and it hit home. But it was so much more than me grasping an idea, I actually doubt that I grasped it at all. That moment was so significant because I *experienced* this idea of a loving God. I have no idea if my mom knew how meaningful this moment was for me. This was my introduction to the Creator, not grasping doctrines and concepts but an introduction to experiencing a love so vast it felt like infinity.

This was my first step toward being a full-fledged Scarcello. Soon after this, my initiation would be complete.

St. Rush

There's two sides to every coin. Politics and religion were marriage partners in my family. I wasn't raised to interpret one without the other. In our home, there was only one acceptable political party—and it wasn't the one Bill and Hillary Clinton belonged to. Growing up I vividly remember my dad loving conservative figures like Bill O'Reilly and Sean Hannity. There were actually only about three or four things ever on our TV, and when it wasn't sports, *Barney* or *The Land Before Time*, it was Fox News.

We have a picture of me as a little kid kissing the TV screen while Rush Limbaugh was on it. I did this because my dad told me, "Always listen to Rush. There's God, there's Mommy and Daddy, and then there's Rush Limbaugh." I knew who Rush Limbaugh was before I knew feces and Clintons were not the same things. I know some people who would call that child abuse, but my family just called it my christening.

These were the constructs passed down to me as a child. They were sacred and fundamental to us and they shaped how I would view the world for many years to come. I was quite content with my constructs of being loved by God and being a Republican, even if I had no idea what the latter meant. But it would not take long before the church world would remove the confidence I held in the love God had for me.

What the Hell?

When I was seven, my family was attending a large church in Eugene, Oregon. As with many evangelical churches, big and small, this church hosted a yearly Vacation Bible School (or, for the indoctrinated, VBS) every summer. This is something one of my agnostic friends would later go on to call "Camp Brainwash." For those of you who don't know, VBS is where churches try to bring in as many kids as they can and immerse them in that

PART I: BEAUTIFUL FAITH SHACKLED IN SHAME

church's theology of God and the Bible. The type of church you attend will determine what is taught at VBS. Now, for the record, I don't share the same sentiments about VBS as my agnostic friends. I think VBS can be a wonderful thing. Though, as with anything involving church, it also has potential to be a horrifying experience. Here's what I mean.

My cousin was in town visiting from Seattle in the summer of 1999. Together we ventured to my church's VBS. It was pretty standard stuff in the beginning. We played games, ate goldfish, and drank apple juice. We listened to a Bible story as the sweet old lady used a blue felt board with Caucasian Bible characters, and we had worship, getting down to such gems as "I Can Sing of Your Love Forever" and "Our God is an Awesome God." Church business as usual, right? Well, things took a weird and twisted turn.

We were ushered into this large classroom upstairs. Once we were all seated on the floor, a man in a black turtleneck (this was 1999) stood in front of us. Later I found out he was the children's pastor, the man who was directing that year's VBS. He said, "We are going to go in the room next door. Once I open the door, we will enter a dark maze. No matter what happens, follow me through this maze. In there you will see people tempting you with candy to lead you away from me, but I promise if you don't listen to them, and you follow me, you will get a much bigger reward than the candy."

You think you know where he's going with this, right? I thought so too.

The man led myself, my cousin, and about ten other kids to the maze. It was dark and cold, and I could tell the maze was made of black fabric and cardboard. We moved quickly through the maze, and sure enough there were people throughout the ordeal temping us with bite-size Smarties and Snickers to not follow the man anymore. They were teenagers, much cooler than me. I really wanted to listen to them. They said things like, "It's a trap. Don't do it! We've got candy." Many kids fell for the candy. Weaklings. I resisted. I figured if they were offering bite-size Snickers this guy is bound to give us king-size Reese's Peanut Butter Cups to symbolize the reward we get for our faithful devotion to Christ.

When we finally got to the center of the maze, it was pitch black and felt enormous.

We sat in quiet for a moment.

Then all of a sudden a red strobe light in the center of the room turned on and loud haunted house music started. The walls of this cardboard room were covered with tinfoil that had red and yellow flames painted on it, and heaters inside the room turned on making it unbearably hot.

Plot twist: we were in hell. Because 1990s evangelicalism.

The man held a big flashlight under his face and let out a loud, maniacal laugh. He then shouted in a cackling voice:

"You fools! My name is Satan and I am the Father of Lies! Those Christians tried to lead you away from this path. They warned you it was a trap and offered you a reward! But you didn't listen! Now you are in hell with me forever! I will let my rats feast on your flesh forever. Your suffering will never cease!"

Kids around me started crying. One kid started repenting of his sins, asking God for another chance right then. I was furious I didn't get my king-size Reese's. Another kid said, "That's not fair! We didn't know you were Satan! You cheated!" Another yelled, "This lesson doesn't even make sense!"

She was right. What were we supposed to learn? Never trust a children's pastor?

The man screamed, "Silence, fools! Now you will be with me forever! I will bathe you in the lakes of fire! I will throw you into bottomless pits! Your suffering will never end!" And then he let out a hideously loud laugh.

Kids went from crying to sobbing. One girl started screaming. At this point I was getting mad at this stunt and I began to wonder if this guy might actually be the devil.

The black fabric on the top of the center of the maze lifted and the lights came on. The man stood up and I was dumb enough to expect an apology. He took a second to look at the crying children, and then he proceeded to say in a calm voice:

"Today you were given an opportunity to see what your future will be like if you don't accept Jesus into your heart. Very few people get such a blessing. God will send you straight to hell and Satan will make good on everything you just heard him say if you don't repent. You must repent and sin no more, because what if God comes in his wrath while you're in the middle of sinning? You will be banished to Hell forever. Now, how many of you want to accept Jesus Christ as your Lord and Savior?"

And you better believe every hand in that room went up so fast you could hear an actual *whoosh* sound.

PART I: BEAUTIFUL FAITH SHACKLED IN SHAME

Shalom vs. Shame

My first interaction with God did not involve threats of being eaten alive by rats or being bathed in fire, nor did it guarantee a reward for saying the right words. Even if those things were part of the conversation with my mom, they're not what sticks with me to this day. My first God encounter was filled with a sense of warm wholeness and an awfully keen awareness of my value. There is a Hebrew word that captures what my first interaction with God was like. The word is *Shalom*. *Shalom* is most commonly translated as "peace." While this isn't an erroneous translation, it is a significant oversimplification. The Jewish language has fewer words than the English language so a lot of Hebrew words carry concepts instead of simplistic definitions. *Shalom* is one of those words. *Shalom* is the absence of conflict. It is wholeness. It is this mysterious awareness that things are exactly as they were always intended to be. *Shalom* is found in those moments of prayer and worship where you are keenly aware of the living connection established between you and the Creator. *Shalom* is a group of friends who get a night away together and let loose playing *Rock Band* on the Xbox late into the night. *Shalom* is cuddling with your significant other on the couch while you watch a good movie. For me it's the smell of freshly ground coffee in the morning or sharing a bottle of decent scotch with friends around a table. It is rare, but it is available to anyone. In his book, *It's Not What You Think*, author Jefferson Bethke writes about *Shalom*, saying:

> *Shalom* is when you hear or see something and can't quite explain it, but you know it's calling and stirring something deep inside of you. *Shalom* is a sunset, that sense of exhaustion yet satisfaction from a hard day's work, creating art that is bigger than itself. *Shalom* is enemies being reconciled by love. *Shalom* is when you are dancing to the rhythm of God's voice.

That moment with my mom—more specifically that moment with God—was *Shalom*. And I've been living for moments such as that ever sense.

Before my time in the maze, I never thought of God as anything other than the Truest Love. It wasn't the promise of heaven or the threat of hell that compelled me as a child; it was this idea that there was a Being out there who loved me with a greater love than that of even my mom. It's easy now for me to look back at my experience in the wannabe Hell House with morbid entertainment. But something very destructive took place in me as that happened. A seed was planted in me that grew into a tree, and I've been trying to uproot it ever since. It was a tree of shame, and its fruit was self-destruction. All of a sudden God felt distant and angry, disapproving and disappointed. Looking back on that experience I realize it was the first of many that caused me to believe, on some level, I was fundamentally detestable to God. I was convinced God didn't love me as I was and that I had to find a way to clean myself up before I could experience *shalom* again.

Over the years, we began attending a different church, but the idea of God I had been absorbing continued to drift further and further away from the God I had experienced. All of a sudden, my goal was to appease God, not to love God. After that moment in my mother's room I remember just marveling at the majesty of God. I would talk to him about everything: about how I hoped there would be Happy Meals in heaven, about bugs, trucks, and the mystical experience of eating a doughnut. After the tour of hell, and a few years of first-through-fifth-grade Sunday school classes, the only talking I ever did with God was begging him in fear and trembling not to throw me into hell forever.

No love. No *shalom*. Just fear, shame, and a lot of anxiety.

This is not to say my Sunday school teachers only ever talked about wrath and judgment—I remember hearing about God's love and grace plenty—but unconditional love and unmerited grace were never as convincing to me as paying the price of hell for my sins.

This was more the fault of basic human biology than it was my Sunday school teachers. Our brains latch themselves onto pain like a bear trap. When the human brain experiences something negative, it latches onto that negativity. Our brains are designed to instantaneously trap fear, pain, and shame. This is our biological alarm system. We naturally hold on to the negative so we are better equipped to avoid it. This came in handy when we were frequently being chased by tigers or eating poisonous berries in the Paleolithic era, but we don't do those things anymore, so it is just anxiety. The other side of this is the effects of positive moments take actual intention to keep if we don't want to lose their lasting impressions on our brains. I once heard on a podcast (though I could not find which specific one) Franciscan friar Father Richard Rohr recommend that when something beautiful happens in our lives we ought to stop right away for ten to fifteen seconds to take it in and let it leave its imprint on our brains, otherwise it will vanish like it never happened.

PART I: BEAUTIFUL FAITH SHACKLED IN SHAME

So, on some level it does not matter how much you talk to a kid incapable of understanding nuance about the love of God. Any time you paint the picture of a God who is mad at you and must be appeased by your actions or else, you have created a mental connection of God with fear and shame. I'm not advocating we don't tell children how important our actions are or that we should not tell them there are consequences for what we do and do not do; I am saying I lost the God of love to the God of wrath, and I've seen it happen to so many kids. This, I believe, is what Jesus meant when he warned not to "lead one of these little ones astray" (Matt 18:6 NLT).

When I began deconstructing, this experience in the Hell House, along with a few others like it (one time in middle school a youth leader told me every time I masturbated it was like whipping another lash on Christ's broken body), were some of the first things I raged against. Often times I would think to myself, or out loud, or on Facebook, "How dare the church play a part in teaching kids how to hate themselves! Doesn't the world do enough of that?"

My experience is not at all uncommon for those raised in evangelical churches. Well-meaning people think they are teaching kids about sin and its dangers, but it is being done in a way that instills much more shame than gratitude. I cannot tell you how many people start a devastating deconstruction process because of the damaging amounts of shame they were exposed to in church. When we lead someone to believe God's love is something to be earned, whether in our words or our behavior, we diminish the power of the cross.

Sin is destructive. It destroys community, family, beauty, even our humanity. Sin must be taken care of—and it was when Love itself suffered and died on the cross, and in doing so participated in the Great Exchange: surrendering his perfect life and freeing us from the dark powers that held the world in destructive bondage. We practice abhorrent theology when we start with sin management and build our spirituals lives off of that. It is a weak and feeble foundation. Love is the strongest foundation in the world. The shocking and scandalous truth is love is enough. Of course, when I speak of love I am not referring to mere sentimentality, nor am I referring to an affirmation of everything one does because one's value is to be affirmed regardless of what they do. I am referring to the type of love which descends to Hades and returns with the keys of life, a robust and powerful love which knows the best way to live.

There is liberation in the belief that all you need is love, but there is bondage in questioning it. And if shame taught me anything, it was to question my value. This questioning-of-value would be kicked into overdrive when I was twelve years old and realized I wasn't attracted to the gender all my other friends seemed to be attracted to.

CHAPTER THREE

Locked in Secret

"Because true belonging only happens when we present our authentic, imperfect selves to the world, our sense of belonging can never be greater than our level of self-acceptance."
—BRENE BROWN

"If I have sinned, what have I done to you, O Watcher of Humanity? Why make me your target? Am I a burden to you?"
—JOB 7:20 (NLT)

Sheetrock and Zucchini Bread

MY PARENTS CHOSE TO homeschool my brother and me. I never got a satisfactory answer as to why—my parents were not trained or particularly skilled educators—though I imagine it was simply what contemporary Christian parents did at the time. Don't let your children watch *The Simpsons* or *Pokémon*? Check. Don't let your kids read *Harry Potter*? Check. Vote for George Bush, Senior and Junior? Check. Homeschool your children? Check. We seemed to be firing on all early 2000s evangelical cylinders. Although, perhaps they simply feared the trials and temptations a public-schooled life would bring their children.

My dad worked in construction by hanging sheetrock. My brother and I would wait in anticipation every day for his return home from work. He'd come in and sweep us up in his arms. He always smelled of drywall and caulking, so to this day the smell of a construction site fills me with a sense of comfort. My dad was enigmatic to me growing up. I was a child with simple categories and my dad was not a simple man. On the one hand, he did manual labor my whole life, was staunchly conservative, obsessed with college football (he was an Oregon State Beavers fan; it broke his heart when I decided to cheer for the Oregon Ducks), and the only time in my childhood I saw him cry was when we watched Old Yeller. Yet my dad was not the emotionally obtuse man movies and television would often depict people like him to be. He was not distant, didn't rule the house with anger or rage, and I never questioned his love for me. He always gave hugs, always tucked us in and prayed with us at night, and a day never went by when he didn't tell us he loved us. When Mom would have nights out with her girlfriends or go out of town to visit friends or family, Dad made us instant pancakes for dinner and we watched movies Mom didn't want us to watch. This is where my near obsession with movies began. Not only was I swept away as a kid by movies like *Saving Private Ryan*, *The Patriot*, *Braveheart*, and *Gladiator*, I was enraptured by the idea of doing something sneaky with my dad.

As my dad went to work every day my mom took on the even more difficult task of homeschooling my brother and me. She was so committed to this process that as things got financially tight, or when we wanted to take a vacation to Disneyland, my mom would do a nighttime paper route to supplement the income. My mom was jovial, hilarious, loud, and the life of the party. She liked crafts, Martha Stewart, *Law and Order* (especially *SVU*), shock humor, and cooking. She was famous (in our circles at least) for her zucchini bread. She and her brother, my Uncle Ryan, had an ongoing feud as to who made better shortbread cookies. As a kid, there was no one I knew who embodied fun or nurturing love more than her.

My mom made people feel safe and wanted. Even while functioning within a religious movement that was quick to reject people who didn't fit the mold, my mom seemed to give love and companionship to whoever was around her. We were Republican Pentecostals who seemed to check off all of our tribe's major boxes, but I was not raised alongside people exclusively in this framework. My parents had friends who were not Christians, friends who voted for Al Gore and later John Kerry, friends who were former hippies and opposed the Iraq war, friends who attended protests and boycotted Walmart, and friends who were gay.

PART I: BEAUTIFUL FAITH SHACKLED IN SHAME

They're Just . . . Roommates?

Shortly after we moved out of our little duplex, we found a slightly larger house in downtown Springfield, Oregon. It didn't take long for my brother and me to make friends with a neighborhood boy who lived with his mom and her roommate. We loved being at their house. They had a room full of movies I knew I wasn't allowed to watch, but I would sit in that room and analyze their cases, longing for the day I could start watching them. There was a trampoline in their backyard, nondiet soda in their fridge, and practical jokes to spare. We loved being at their house, and my parents loved spending time with our friend's mom and roommate.

After about a year of friendship I must have been nine years old, and something dawned on me as strange. I noticed in my friends three-bedroom house that he had his own room, the movies and computer had their own room, and his mom and her roommate shared a room . . . with one queen-sized bed in it. I knew they weren't just roommates, so I confronted my parents. Despite what I had discovered, my mom persisted with the ruse. I knew my mom was lying to me, but I couldn't figure out why. Even after six months to a year later when my dad eventually caved and told me that they were in fact lesbians, I never got an answer as to why my mom lied about it. I've been left to develop a few conclusions on my own about her deceit.

My suspicion is that my parents wanted my brother and I to be raised with the notion that being gay, bisexual, or lesbian was uncomplicatedly sinful. It was a step away from God and not to be associated with. My parents clearly had slightly more complicated ideas than that as they spent time with this couple regularly, but they also seemed committed to making sure my brother and I would not have a nuanced view on the matter, even going to the point of deceiving us about it. Either way, by the time I figured out these neighbors whom I loved were lesbians it was made clear to me that *they* were not *us*, even if they felt enough like us. I'm not sure this is the message my mom meant to convey, but what I picked up through her white lie was this: what they were doing was wrong, so wrong in fact, that my parents had to make up a lie just to cover up even being associated with them.

It is important to remember their context. My parents were more charitable toward the couple across the street in the nineties than plenty of Christians I know would be today. They did not demonstrate homophobia with their speech or by avoiding the couple. In this time, the church was hardly being equipped with ways to have these conversations with graciousness and understanding, and my parents did better than most probably would have. Still, the fixation of fear and suspicion the evangelical church held toward the queer community did not allow my parents space to handle this in as healthy a way as they could have. Remember, we were fiery Pentecostals with roots in the Assemblies of God, where they were exposed to a lot of the teachings and followers of Jimmy Swaggart. I remember watching a sermon of Jimmy's from the early 2000s where he proudly boasted that if a homosexual ever talked to him he would punch them right in the face. I don't remember where I first saw that clip, but I was young enough for it to leave quite the imprint on my mind.

I do not remember the first time I learned our faith did not affirm the LGBTQ+ community. I do not know if it was my parents, the talking heads on Fox News, or church that broke it to me. Homosexuality being a sin has been ingrained in me for as long as I can remember. Before I knew greed, lust, pride, idolatry, or violence went against the teachings of Christ, I knew it was wrong to be gay. And the fact I knew our theology on homosexuality before I knew our theology on any of the aforementioned subjects should tell you everything you need to know about why there is such a tense backlash against conservative evangelicalism in this cultural moment. Through my mom's well-intended fib, I learned being gay was a different kind of sin than lying or stealing. This was a sin that would lead the people who associate with you to deny knowing you . . . it did not just lead you to shame; it led your friends and family to shame.

So, when I turned twelve years old, and I experienced my first crush, I did not get to giddily tell my friends or parents about it, because my first crush was on a boy . . . and I thought my life was over.

So, this is Love?

I had my first true crush when I was twelve years old. He was a friend I made at church. I don't remember exactly what it was that first drew me to him, only that I always wanted to be around him. There was not anything intrinsically sexual about my feelings toward him at the start. It seemed harmless enough, and because I had not really encountered sexuality it did not raise too many red flags. Not to mention I did not yet understand that I could have these types of feelings for a boy, so there was no way to have known in the moment what was happening to me. Things got substantially more complicated when I had a romantic dream about the boy. I remember waking up so afraid I could not move. Even now recalling the moment I sense a sick feeling in the pit of my stomach, not because I carry any intentional shame over it—after all this was something happening to me not something I was pursuing—but because the fear was so profound I still feel it echoing in my chest. *What am I becoming?* I thought. This fear led me to cut off as much connection with this boy as possible. No more hanging out, no more sitting next to each other at church, no more talking to him.

And it worked for a while. A few months went by with no dreams. It hurt to not be near him, but that feeling soon faded. I never had to acknowledge what I was experiencing as a legitimate crush. Additionally, as a way of compensating for the deep fear I was experiencing, I attempted to feign interest in girls. I even met one or two in my middle school years I genuinely liked. However, no matter how much I tried, I never seemed to desire female attention as much as my friends did. I never enjoyed kissing girls as much as they did either. I just figured I was going to be a late bloomer and would eventually grow into those things.

At Church Camp of All Places

Summer came and we went to church camp. At camp, this boy and I were placed in a cabin together. We reconnected and I instantly started experiencing all the emotion toward him I thought I had shaken off. It terrified me. Thankfully, we rarely did anything just the two of us. We were part of a bigger "squad" that swam in the lake, pulled pranks on other campers, and got camp girlfriends together. I even got a few camp girlfriends, though I admittedly had no idea what to do with them. In the evenings, after emotional worship services and night games, we were sent back to our cabins. Inexplicably, we were a cabin full of middle-school boys with no leader in it. I don't know what the leaders of this camp were thinking. The first couple nights my friends and I would stay up way too late. We would tell stories of all the times we *swear to God* we saw ghosts in real life (I'm sure none of us were lying about that). We would tell stories of our first kisses, greatest pranks, and fights we got into at school. We talked about friends we knew who were already smoking and having sex, and swore we would never do those things, though most of us would eventually do those things just a couple years later. Looking back on those nights with sixteen years of perspective I can't help but notice how bright and warm those memories are.

On the third night, however, our cabin was exhausted after two nearly sleepless nights in a row. Most of the cabin fell right to sleep except for me and this boy. We sat together on my bunk and talked for hours. Serious talk. As serious of a conversation as a couple of almost-thirteen-year-olds could have. He shared with me about how his parents were fighting more, and how afraid he was that they might divorce. He had tears in his eyes, then he rested his head on my shoulder and I put my arm around him. We sat there for a moment, and I was filled with a thousand different feelings. I was sad for my friend and his situation, elated at the intimacy we were finally sharing, terrified at how much I loved it, and guilty for feeling anything positive because this was happening while he was in pain. Then he took his head off of my shoulder and looked me in the eyes. He leaned in, kissed me on the lips, and held himself there. And when he didn't pull himself away, I knew I was done for. That night he returned to his own bunk and I laid in my bed, eyes wide open and full of tears, repeating the phrase over and over again in my head, *What have I done?*

It would be years before I ever talked to that boy again. Shortly after this camp his family left our church.

A New Mission

I remember the days leading up to that night with the boy and the days immediately after in two different hues. If the days leading up to it were full of warm and bright colors, the days after were full of cold and muted colors. I woke up the next morning feeling as if all the life in me had left. A first experience that is usually the highlight of any young boy's middle-school career had confirmed my most horrifying suspicions, and I thought the most dreaded four words I could imagine: *I am not straight.*

These four words should not be the four words to ruin a young person's life. I'm not sure there is ever an easy way to come to this realization, but it doesn't take a progressive, gay-marriage-affirming theologian to know this thought should not lead a child to believing they are a monster and their life is over. But at that moment the four words meant so much more than just the revelation of my sexual orientation. *I am not straight* also meant was no longer acceptable to my friends and family. If the people who loved me most knew the real me, I would be totally and utterly rejected. I could not shake the belief that I was no longer a person capable of being loved by God. People chose to be gay, or so I believed at the time, and if I experience this then on some deep and depraved level, I am choosing a life apart from God.

My life had a new mission: no matter what, at all costs, *hide*. My parents, friends, and church could never find out. And maybe, just maybe, if I fought this off long enough, God would see that I really did not want it and would free me from it.

In her book *The Gifts of Imperfection*, Dr. Brene Brown talks about the three things shame needs to grow: silence, secrecy, and judgment. She says if you had a petri dish, and you put those three ingredients in there, shame would grow rapidly. My return home from that camp marked the beginning of a life defined by shame. Silence and secrecy became my vow, and judgment on myself and others with similar experiences would be my tool to stay diligent (it didn't work).

When I got home from camp and saw my parents for the first time, even when they hugged me, I felt a million miles away from them. I remember excusing myself to my bedroom and weeping. My mom and dad were the definitive pictures of nurturing and protective love, and I wanted nothing more than to tell them. But I convinced myself if I did, I would lose them. The only thing I wanted more than to tell my parents was to not risk being rejected by them. So, hiding became the most important, exhausting, and consistent work I had to do.

Shortly after camp, a friend and I were hanging out. We were sitting on the steps outside our church on a warm summer evening. I don't remember what sparked the conversation, but he asked me a question I'll never forget. He said: "Tony, if I were gay, would you still be my friend?"

I panicked. *He knows*, I thought. You see, this friend had been in the cabin that night. I feared he was awake when things transpired and thought he might be testing me. I was afraid if I said "yes" it would confirm my secret to him and he would tell people about me. I had to protect myself at all costs. So, I answered, "No way man, that's gross."

Later on in high school, I learned this friend deeply struggled with his sexual identity. I can only imagine the damage my self-preserving response did to him and his sense of self. To this day it is one of my biggest regrets.

No Escape

Weeks turned to months, and every night I prayed for God to set me free. Sometimes I would weep and pray for hours, sometimes just a few patient minutes before bed. Nothing changed. In fact, things only got worse. As puberty was working overtime, so were my hormones. I watched porn with some friends for the first time, and I sort of liked it. *If I like this straight people stuff on video then maybe I'll be able to like it in real life*, I thought. That thought lasted all but a few weeks until I discovered there were several types of pornography for me to access. The more I watched porn, the more my shame built up, the further away God seemed, and the less likely it felt that I would be able to live as the man I wanted to be.

When I was fourteen years old the nightmare of developing romantic feelings for another male friend started all over again, only this time lines were crossed and doors were opened which led to an even greater propensity for fear, shame, and self-hatred. The cycle continued with this young man for years. We never spoke of our physical relationship to each other or anyone else (at least on my end of things). We never spoke of any feelings to each other. We just stayed with the routine we had established. The cycle continued even as I transitioned from being home-schooled to attending our public high school. We barely spoke at school, but it didn't change how we spent our time together outside of school. By the time I got to high school, I had experienced physical encounters with two different boys whom I knew from church, boys who I would have never guessed experienced same-sex attraction. It made me think, *Well, maybe everybody is gay. Maybe everybody's gay and nobody's talking about it.*

I loved this friend, not necessarily in a romantic sense, but we had a genuine connection. Even though I deeply valued our relationship it only served as an arsenal for the war being waged in my thought-life. Every moment of intimacy with this friend led me further into self-hatred and depression. When I was fifteen years old, I realized there was no escaping this. For two years I prayed for God to take it away and it was only getting worse. The God I had experienced in my mom's room when I was four years old was dying, and I was dying with him. And the world around me was not exactly growing more queer-friendly. As George Bush Jr. ran for his second term, gay marriage was being heavily debated. While I'm sure this was a liberating experience for those outside the church, inside the church us closeted folk were suffering as pastors and Fox News pundits grew more aggressive in their homophobic rhetoric. The "love the sinner, hate the sin" rhetoric only confirmed to me and countless other people who could not change their struggles that we were detestable.

I had come to the conclusion that my life was only going one of two ways:

1. I would fully give into my sexual desires. I would lose everything and everyone I loved. I would lose my family, friends, church, and Jesus.
2. Or, I could end it immediately. And dying was more bearable to me than breaking the hearts of my loved ones. I genuinely believed it would be better for me to be dead than for me to be queer.

It was only a matter of time before all that shame and pain within me would attempt to destroy me. At fifteen years old, on an evening when my parents were out, I tried to drink a bottle of bleach in our bathroom. I didn't get much down before I found myself bent over the toilet vomiting it up. I went to bed that night sick, sad, alone, and feeling more ashamed than ever, but I decided to take that moment as a sign that God wanted me alive and vowed not to try to kill myself again.

CHAPTER FOUR

Nothing Stands between Us

"Self-rejection is the greatest enemy of the spiritual life because it contradicts the sacred voice that calls us the 'Beloved.' Being the Beloved expresses the core truth of our existence."
—HENRI NOUWEN

"I have loved you with an everlasting love. With my unfailing love, I have drawn you to myself."
—JEREMIAH 31:3 (NLT)

From Bad to Worse

A FEW MONTHS LATER I had learned the secret to numbing myself. I couldn't afford to feel anymore. Alcohol, food, and marijuana were all ways to numb my pain. Eventually, though, the numbness would become more devastating than the depression. When I stopped trying to numb myself I could not escape the devastating feeling of nothingness. See, even in depression there would be glimpses of light breaking through the dark. While depressed I could still experience joy in late-night drives with friends, going to movies with my dad, or acting in a play. But when numb, no light or joy could break through.

At this time, I discovered one of my friends from school was cutting herself. When I asked why she did it, she said "I don't really know. I just know when I'm done doing it I feel better." So, I decided to start cutting.

PART I: BEAUTIFUL FAITH SHACKLED IN SHAME

The first night I took a box cutter out of my dad's tool shed, and began digging little cuts into my arm. It hurt, and sometimes I cut too deep, but it did provide a temporary experience of release from the numbness. Later I learned the cutting released endorphins into my head, the pleasure hormone, so I kept doing it.

I need no greater evidence of the evil at work in our world than the fact that sometimes teenagers mutilate their bodies just to feel something.

Months later, the cuts on my arms and legs became too difficult to hide. My mom caught on and begged me to tell her what was going on. I just told her I was sad for a little while, but that I would stop. I didn't stop. I couldn't stop. Days when I tried not to cut were filled with full-blown panic attacks. Add to the mix the reality that the difficulties of life were not confined to my closeted sexuality. During all these years of struggling, my mom endured a gastric-bypass surgery that went terribly wrong. The repercussions of her botched surgery led to several years' worth of further surgeries in an attempt to rectify the problem. All that time on the operating table and in recovery left her with a nasty OxyContin dependency. For those who don't know, OxyContin is a painkiller that gives the user a high just as potent, if not more so in some cases, than heroin. She started off using the pills to ease her pain, but as time went on, and as doctors recklessly prescribed them to her, she started using them because she was addicted.

Looking back on this time, it is not hard to see why I was in so much emotional turmoil. My world was falling apart. I could not live with myself because of my deep-seated shame. I did not have a single relationship that truly saw me for who I was. I was lying all the time to everyone around me. I had made so many self-destructive choices that I could not fathom God having any patience for me at this point. And when my mom wasn't sober, my paragon of nurturing love was replaced with a bumbling and sometimes abusive shell of who she was.

I could not take it anymore. I decided if God wasn't going to rescue me, I was no longer bound to the vow I made to him. On May 8th, 2008, I snuck into my parents' room while they slept and found my dad's revolver in the top drawer of his dresser. I went into my bedroom and sat there with the gun on my lap. I knew I wanted to pull the trigger, it was just a matter of gaining the courage to do it.

Psalm 5

I sat on my bed, thinking of my mother's face as she would come into my bedroom to wake me up for school the next morning. I wished there was a way for me to explain to her it wasn't her fault. I wished I could tell my dad that I never felt a lack of love from him. I wanted there to be a way to convey to them I did not want to die, but I could not go through the shame anymore. And I (thought I) knew if they found out, my shame would be their shame. Suicide was the only way I knew how to contain the problem.

I know now that my parents would have found a way to cope with my news, maybe they would have even helped me sort through everything. I know it would have been a tough blow to them, but they would have done anything to keep me from dying. Shame had so distorted my sense of reality that there was no reasoning with me. Remember the three things shame needs to grow: silence, secrecy, and judgment. I had those three components in spades, and my shame had grown beyond sustainable heights. So, I sat there with a loaded gun. I recalled the first time my dad took me shooting with this gun, when I was ten years old. I remember shooting glass bottles and paper targets. I remembered his gentle and protective love. I knew my dad would blame himself. There was no avoiding it. I had to accept that.

At around 1:00 am I had enough internal resolution to figure my parents would eventually be okay. Then my cell phone started vibrating, I looked at it and saw a friend of mine was calling. This friend was in California visiting family. *What was he doing calling me this late on a school night?* I answered, worrying something would be wrong. We exchanged hellos, and I asked him why he was calling me so late. What he said next floored me.

"Tony, I was up playing video games with my brother, and I just knew God was telling me to pray for you. So, I went outside and started praying for you, and I started crying..."

His voice was shaking. He was still crying.

"So, I got my bible and I opened it to Psalm 5. Do you know what Psalm 5 says, Tony? I need you to grab your Bible and read it with me."

So, I grabbed my Bible off of my night stand, and told him I got it. He told me to read verses one through three. I had an NLT translation, and this is what it said:

"O Lord, hear me as I pray;
pay attention to my groaning.

PART I: BEAUTIFUL FAITH SHACKLED IN SHAME

Listen to my cry for help, my King and my God,
For I pray to no one but you.
Listen to my voice in the morning, Lord.
Each morning I bring my requests to you and wait patiently."

After I got done reading there was silence on the other end of the phone . . . then my friend said, "Tony, I don't know what's going on, but I know something is up. And God hears you. Don't stop praying. Wait patiently, because I promise, your rescue is coming."

I was in shock. I did not know what to say, and my innate distrust of vulnerability prevented me from telling him in that moment how badly I needed to hear that. I thanked him, and told him promptly I needed to go. I couldn't identify what I was feeling in that moment, but I knew the emotion was rumbling in me like a volcano. I could not stay still. I set the gun on my night stand, and got up to get a drink of water from our kitchen. What I saw next managed to both scare the hell out of me and save my life.

At the Cross Where I First Saw the Light

As I walked out of my bedroom and into our hallway, I noticed on the wall in our dining room was the large image of a luminescent cross. It was big, bright, beautiful, and ghostly. I freaked out and almost woke my parents, but then I noticed where it was coming from. I looked at the window across from our dining room and saw my mom's glass cross sitting on the window sill. The porchlight was shining through it, and created the beautiful spectacle on our wall. I calmed down, but only for a moment. I had

> I see all of you. Every dark corner you try to keep hidden is in plain sight to me. I love all of you.

been in this dining room many times without seeing this cross illuminated on our wall. Maybe I had just been ignorant, maybe I was hallucinating, maybe something holy was taking place, or maybe it was all of the above. Then I heard God speak to me. Not audibly, but to my soul. It was as if God downloaded the words into my head and heart. And I'll never forget what he said.

"I see all of you. Every dark corner you try to keep hidden is in plain sight to me. I love all of you. I died on the cross to show the extent of my love for you. I left my glory to bring you to glory. And I promise you, if you dedicate your whole life to me, I will give you a life that is thrilling and fulfilling."

I began weeping, and in my thoughts, I protested: "But God, how can I follow you and love you while struggling with this? How can I trust you if you won't take it away?"

To which God seemed to reply, "Nothing stands between us. Not that or anything else. Just follow me, and trust my love. You will be okay."

I fell to my knees in tears. I was laid bare, totally exposed and totally loved; something I never thought was possible. The light in my heart was switched on. I did not have to be tormented anymore. It was as if a demon had been exorcised out of my soul, which makes sense, because in some very real ways shame is demonic. My sex drive and orientation did not go away or change. What went away was the oppressive feeling that my life would end in ruin. I was in the presence of God, and was given permission to move forward without having all the answers.

John Mark McMillan released a song in 2017 called "Nothing Stands between Us," and as you can imagine when I first heard it I was instantly reduced to a puddle of tears. Make sure to check it out. And then listen to everything else he's ever done.

Maybe it was just a coincidence that my friend called me moments before I was going to kill myself. Maybe it was just good timing that I saw the cross on the wall. Maybe seeing the cross just sparked those words to come into my head and heart. It's possible.

But here's what I believe in my heart of hearts: that night every clichéd verse and platitude I heard about the love of God became reality to me. I was saved. I was saved from my shame, self-hatred, and my desire to die. I was lost, and then found. The light of God illuminated the darkest corners of my heart, and I was finally free to love and follow Jesus. I was given freedom, but it looked different than I thought it would. I love how A. J. Swoboda puts it in his book, *The Dusty Ones*, "It turns out that freedom in Christ does not necessarily include freedom spatially, or relationally, or vocationally. More often than not, we will blossom most in those stuck places we'd never want to be or dreamed we'd be in in the first place."

In the season of discovering my sexual orientation the God of love my mom introduced to me when I was young died a slow and painful death in my heart. But in that moment, in my family's dining room, I experienced his brilliant and beautiful resurrection.

PART I: BEAUTIFUL FAITH SHACKLED IN SHAME

The One Thing I Could Not Do

I regularly refer to that moment in my dining room as the moment I got saved. Not because I wasn't a Christian beforehand—I always thought of myself as a Christian—but because it was the first time my life was given a purpose greater than hiding. It wouldn't be long after this experience that I would be gifted with a couple best friends, Jordan and Dennis, to teach me how to follow Jesus. To this day, through our studying, living, arguing, and loving, we teach each other what it means to be Jesus followers. And even if I didn't share my secret with them in high school, I have always felt truly seen by them.

Through these relationships, through my new zeal for all things Jesus and Scripture, and through a few adults who took an interest in me, I grew more and more into a confident young man. And I was filled with a *I-will-do-whatever-you-say, go-wherever-you-send-me* passion for Jesus. And I meant it. My faith was a blazing fire. Nothing was more exciting and important to me than Jesus. I still struggled with what it would look like for me to fall in love, fought shame over my temptations and indulgences, and feared rejection if anyone found out my secret. But for that season, being seen and accepted by God was enough. It was enough for me to move forward, forge a path for myself, and invest in meaningful relationships.

As I began reading my Bible more, I started reading verses like Romans 8:1: "There is no condemnation for those who are in Christ Jesus." My shame told me this could not be true, but my experience with Jesus told me it was. As I grew in my new friendships, I also knew in my heart, even if I did not have the language for it, that I was created to function in transparent love and belonging. I would never fully experience being known and loved while keeping this secret.

I began to desire the opportunity to tell someone. I knew it would give me room to breathe. I began asking God for the words and the opportunities to tell my family. However, finding the right moment seemed impossible. In 2008, the recession put my dad out of work at the same time my mom fell deeper into her addiction, to the point where she was visibly wasting away.

One evening I had a few friends over to stay the night. The three of us decided to watch one of our favorite movies, *Saving Private Ryan*. We started the movie late, and my two friends fell asleep shortly after the Normandy scene (because you always stay awake long enough to watch the Normandy scene). One of these friends laid his head on my shoulder as they fell asleep. The lying of his head on my shoulder was completely innocent. I continued to watch the movie when I felt a violent tug on my ear. The tug hurt so much it frightened me. I turned around to see my mom standing there in her bathrobe. She had a firm grimace on her face, and furiously gestured for me to follow her to the backyard. I obeyed.

When we got to the backyard I asked my mom what was wrong and she didn't answer. She just glared at me as she lit her cigarette. She was high. After taking in a long puff of smoke, she exhaled and started crying. "Mom, what's wrong? Why are we out here?"

"Do you like that boy?" she said, her voice shaking.

"Of course, I do, Mom. He's my friend." I said, dodging the question I knew she was asking me. Clearly my mom had been suspecting something was "off" with me in this area, and saw my friend asleep on my shoulder as her chance to confront me. I'm not sure having this conversation in the haze of her Oxy high was the right time, but here we were.

"You know what I mean, Anthony!" she snapped. She only ever called me Anthony when I was in trouble. "Do you have a crush on him? Are you gay?"

Something about the way she said the word "gay" informed me that this would not be the best time to confirm her suspicions.

"No, Mom, I don't like him like that." I said while inwardly begging God to make her believe me.

She looked a little relieved.

"There are a lot of things you can do, honey. You can get high, get drunk, get in fights . . . Those are all wrong but I can work with them. The one thing you cannot do to me is be gay," she said to me, slurring her words and hardly able to stand still thanks to the narcotics pumping through her system. Rage bellowed within me.

I was angry at the way in which I was forced to watch my mom slowly disappear. I was angry I had been putting up with her stoned ramblings for years now. I was angry my deepest struggle would somehow be interpreted as something I *did* to her. I was angry I had to stay hiding in shame, while most of our friends and family knew my mom was struggling with a drug addiction and it didn't seem to faze them. But most of all, I was angry my mother just confirmed every insecurity and fear I held since I realized this about myself—this was the one thing I could not do to her. Only now I knew something I did not know before: God accepted me. God loved me.

PART I: BEAUTIFUL FAITH SHACKLED IN SHAME

God wanted me, and every messy struggle I experienced. Who had a right to be more frustrated with me more than God? I now knew intuitively I was worthy of acceptance and belonging. And the fact that my own mother would not be offering those things to me if I were to show her the deepest parts of myself set me off. So, in a fit of rage I replied, "Get off the (insert explicative here) drugs, Mom."

I stormed back into the TV room.

She went back to bed without bothering me. I knew it would be a long time before I could tell anyone, if that time was ever going to come. I resolved to let this piece of myself remain a secret.

NOTHING STANDS BETWEEN US

A Letter to My Younger Self

Dear Tony,

I have been thinking about you a lot lately. Today, I remembered the day you went to the casting board at Springfield High School and read that you had been cast in your dream role as Oscar Madison in *The Odd Couple*. You went into the bathroom, and cried tears of joy for the first time in years. Later, you're going to win an award voted on by your peers for this performance, and it will be the highlight of your theater experience. Your mom's addiction is getting worse, and often times spirals into abuse toward you and your brother. You were told earlier that your family couldn't keep up on the payments for their house, and soon you will be living in the attic of some friends. Just before this, the boy you are in love with started to pick up on your feelings toward him. He got scared and stopped talking to you. You don't know this now, but some day the world will be a safer place for people like you. You will fall in love a few more times, and you will meet friends who don't reciprocate your feelings, but they will continue to love you like a brother, and you too will soon love them like family.

Your external world is falling apart but you feel more alive than you have since before you knew of your struggle. God is in you, and you can feel that. You get up every morning an hour before school to read your Bible and listen to worship music, and the Spirit fills you with the stability missing in your life. You have a new friend, Jordan, and you don't know it yet but he's going to continue to be your best friend even twelve years later. Soon you will meet a boy named Dennis, and he will be the first person you ever tell about your struggle. He will love you and embrace you. You still battle shame over your sexuality, and wonder why God won't lift what feels like a curse. You are afraid for your mom and your heart breaks for your dad. He is losing his job, home, and wife. You still get panic attacks over whether or not you will die alone, ever fall in love with a woman, or become a father. You are afraid that the preachers are right, and maybe God really is ashamed of you. But the Spirit is present, giving you life, and you know it.

Someday you will fall in love with a woman, truly and sincerely. She will light up your world in ways you never knew possible by becoming your wife. She will be in your space during the darkest times of your life, and she will light up your soul. But that doesn't mean God has changed your sexual orientation. You will fight, struggle, and learn how to live as a queer man married to the girl of your dreams who follows Jesus faithfully. Someday

PART I: BEAUTIFUL FAITH SHACKLED IN SHAME

you will tell your story, your whole story, and the people you love most will lean into you, not pull away from you. You will speak at churches, youth events, retreats, camps, and college groups. You will tell your story, the story about God showering you with love and truth when all you knew was shame and lies. You will learn God doesn't need to change how you experience sexuality to truly love you. You will tell other LGBTQ+ people this, and they will weep in your arms because it's the gospel they need to hear.

As I grew up I learned there was a price to be paid for all of the hiding you did. I feel exposed and weak whenever I choose vulnerability. I put up walls and wear masks around the safest people in my life, and I think it will take years more for me to learn how to stop hiding. But God is good, and has sent me safe and gracious people whose love tears down those walls and pulls off that mask. Still, choosing authenticity is a grueling choice I have to make every day, because you learned to lie to everyone, all the time, for our entire adolescence. But this is the most important thing I need to tell you: Tony, I am not mad at you. You are trying everything you can to stay alive. You are taking the only options you have available to you. And I'm so proud of how strong you are. You are a survivor and are not easily broken. Right now, you are so scared and you dislike yourself so much, but all your hiding and fronting will not prevent your gentle kindness and compassion from sneaking out. This compassion and kindness that you try to replace with aggression and humor are your greatest strengths.

Hang in there, kid. You have an incredible life to live ahead of you. For now, just take a deep breath, close your eyes, and rest in the fact that you are loved with a Divine love, your value is not determined by what you do or who you're attracted to, and that twelve years from now the twenty-eight-year-old version of yourself is going to write you a letter to let you know how proud he is of you, and how much he loves you.

Grace and peace to you.

—Tony

CHAPTER FIVE

Church

"Faith, doubt, humility, and confidence-this is the stuff and substance of theology at its best. Swagger, smugness and certainty-this is the stuff and substance of theology at its worst."
—AUSTIN FISCHER

"You know my pedigree: a legitimate birth, circumcised on the eighth day; an Israelite from the elite tribe of Benjamin, a strict and devout adherent to God's law; a fiery defender of my religion."
—PHILIPPIANS 3:5-6 (MSG)

Path

I NEVER PUT MUCH stock into the word "calling" when I was in high school. My passions were fairly limited: Jesus, my friends, and acting. Acting was what made me come alive. There wasn't a thing I loved more in the world. I took every opportunity, no matter how stupid the play or small the part, to do it. And, if you believe my friends and family, I was pretty decent for a high schooler.

In the early zeal of my newfound love for Jesus, Jordan and I led a Bible study on campus. We had lots of people coming, and plenty of teachers and students alike asked if I would be pursuing the ministry after high school. I sharply corrected them: "I'm going to New York or L.A. and I'm giving this acting thing a shot."

PART I: BEAUTIFUL FAITH SHACKLED IN SHAME

Clearly, God had other plans for me, thankfully, too, because I do not think I would have made it very long in either of those cities.

In the summer before my senior year I was attending my last church camp as a student. I always loved church camp. I come from a Pentecostal tradition, and no one does church camp like Pentecostals. Speaking in tongues, healings, prophetic words . . . we had the complete package. But more personally, camp was always the place I'd go to remember God had not forgotten me. Whether I was more secure in my standing before the Creator like I was that year, or barely hanging on as I had in the past, God always seemed to come through for me at camp.

It was the last night and I don't remember why I was doing this, but I was on my knees praying and crying (If you didn't cry on the last night of camp, were you even there?). I felt a tap on my shoulder, I looked up, and it was the senior pastor of our church. I always liked him. He brought joy and light into every room he entered. Plus, I'm fairly sure he knew what was going on with my mom because he always went out of his way to show love to my little brother and me.

He asked me to stand up, and I complied. Then he told me he had a word for me. In my circles when somebody tells you they have a word for you, they almost never mean they want to teach you a singular new word. What they mean is they feel God has put something on their heart to share with you. He put his hand on my shoulder and said, "Tony, I saw you on your knees and I started praying for you. Then I got this picture in my head of you speaking to huge crowds, and they were convinced of God's love for them because of what you were saying. God is going to use you in big ways. Stay open to what he may say because you don't want to miss it."

Then he walked away. I was left there and I sensed a movement in my soul. I realized that the thing I wanted most wasn't to go be a movie star, and for as many times as I practiced my Oscar acceptance speech in front of the bathroom mirror while holding a shampoo bottle, even that wasn't the thing I wanted most. I wanted everybody to know that there was good news. Gay, straight, addicted, depressed, anxious, criminal, young and old: there is an unstoppable Force at work in the world that moves its creation toward love and wholeness. Sometimes that movement is rapid, and sometimes it's so slow we can't even see it, but the Spirit is at work. There is a God who wants to bring light to the darkest corners of the soul, and wants to bring liberation to the oppressed. All of creation, indeed our very lives, may seem to be under the curse of sin and death, but God has disarmed death with his resurrection and cleansed sin with his grace. This good news was the best thing I had ever heard, and I hadn't stopped talking about it since I embraced it for myself. I wanted to be a pastor. I knew in that moment my purpose (beyond loving and being loved) was to walk people through the various seasons of life and help them spot grace on the journey. It was to proclaim good news to those living rough stories. I had a path.

> All of creation, indeed our very lives, may seem to be under the curse of sin and death, but God has disarmed death with his resurrection and cleansed sin with his grace. This good news was the best thing I had ever heard, and I hadn't stopped talking about it since I embraced it for myself.

Cage

The following year I graduated high school by the skin of my teeth. Right out of the gate I accepted an internship at the church I grew up in. A year and a half after that I was hired on to lead the middle school group. At first, I did it volunteer, then I started getting a pay check small enough to hardly qualify as part-time. Even though it was a small monthly check, it was a sign from church leadership that they affirmed the path I had started down. It might as well have been millions. I always had other jobs to get by. I usually put in around twenty-five hours a week at the church. Add to that a full-time job (or sometimes two additional part time jobs) and I was easily working sixty-five hours a week while making hardly any money. And I loved every exhausting second of it.

I worked at an amazing church. Every moment not spent with my church on some level was filled with excitement for the next time I got to be there. As my own family felt like it was falling apart, my church filled the void. I felt loved by my lead pastor like I was a son, and much of the staff and church members were like siblings to me. They were my friends, family, and tribe. I looked forward to every staff meeting, Sunday morning service, and event. I was coached to develop spiritual disciplines, gained an ear for Holy Spirit, and learned how to preach the Bible. I was affirmed in my gifts and my callings frequently, with my pastor always reminding me of my potential. I was raised into manhood there. The love and sense of belonging I felt at that church seemed as close to heaven on earth as I could get. I am convinced to this day some of the finest people God ever made call that church their home.

But for all the love and time spent with these beautiful people, I had a secret that felt like shackles on my heart. As every relationship grew in trust and intimacy I was made more aware of the fact I could never reciprocate that level of vulnerability. Once again, I found myself in a situation where I frequently feared being found out. Every time my pastor wanted to meet with me the first thought was always, "He knows."

With my role in leadership, the students I pastored, the people I loved so dearly, and the fact our church held a very strong traditional view on sexuality, I stood to lose more than ever should my secret be found out. So, I mastered the art of locking myself in a glass cage. People could see me, talk to me, and be near me, but they could never see how trapped I really was. I couldn't fathom the idea of losing those people. Just the thought of it made my heart swell with sorrow.

I threw myself into the life of the church as much as humanly possible. And I wanted to be the best pastor I could. When I wanted to be an actor I dove into watching work by ones considered the greats. Al Pacino in *The Godfather Part 2*, Daniel Day Lewis in *There Will Be Blood*, Philip Seymour Hoffman in *Doubt*, Marlon Brando in *On the Waterfront*, Denzel Washington in *Malcolm X*, and many, many others. I immersed myself in their work in hopes of upping my own game. I figured preaching and pastoring should be no different. So, I threw myself into the big, wide world of preaching and theology.

Reformed

My starting place was the book *Crazy Love*, by Francis Chan. I hadn't heard anything about it beforehand, but it was given to me as a graduation gift. My heart was pierced by Francis's direct approach. He made everything seem so clear: God loves me with an insane, out of this world, crazy love; it is only right I should show that crazy love right back. I felt the Christianity I had been living up to that point was neutered and safe. Francis was presenting something to me that was exciting, dangerous, and costly. From Francis, I learned the importance of losing my life and finding it again in Christ. I learned Jesus said some serious things and expected we take them seriously.

After *Crazy Love* and Francis Chan, I discovered Mark Driscoll through a viral video of him on YouTube. He was giving a sermon and screaming from the pulpit about how unmanly it was to hit a woman. Mark was loud, compelling, intelligent, authoritative, and articulate. He took theology out of the textbooks and classrooms and brought it to the streets, making it seem bad-ass. He taught John Calvin and Jonathan Edwards in terms I could understand, and brought the Scriptures to life unlike anyone I had heard. One of my jobs outside of the church was that of a night time newspaper delivery driver, and I would listen to hours of his sermons every night. During this time, I developed rigid categories for what I believed Christianity should be. I was *this close* to getting a tattoo of the term made famous during the reformation in the 1500s, *Sola Scriptura,* which means "Scripture alone." Sitting under Mark Driscoll taught me an imperious approach to the Bible. You didn't have to be kind as long as you were right. Scripture alone was our authority. Scripture alone could discern right from wrong. Scripture alone could teach truth. Scripture alone contains everything you need to know about good, evil, science, history, and humanity. Scripture alone contained the final, inerrant, authoritative word of God. Every question we could possibly have found its answer in Scripture alone.

From Mark, I learned to aggressively call out bad theology. He spoke of a God who was more like the violent and brutal William Wallace than the lamb of God who takes away the sins of the world. "I could never worship someone I can beat up," he would say. God was love but he was also wrath, and if not for his sovereign grace I would burn forever in the fires of hell. I considered anything that made God out to be overly meek, gentle, or kind as teetering on the edge of bad theology. God wasn't interested in being nice, fashionable, or palatable. God was interested in your obedience and his glory. You could talk about forgiveness, but only if you spent enough time talking about why we need forgiving. You could talk about God's love and kindness, but only if you first convinced the listener of how unworthy they were of it. My good news started with really, really bad news. It was as if I was taught to ignore the first two chapters of Genesis. My theology didn't start with being made blessed in God's image, or acknowledging my existence was an expression of God's risky and creative love. My theology started in Genesis 3, where I am cast out of the garden, separated from God's love. I was convinced I and everyone else were sinners in the hands of an angry God. Given the fact I was deeply in the closet, regularly fighting

PART I: BEAUTIFUL FAITH SHACKLED IN SHAME

shame over my secret, it makes sense I would be drawn to Driscoll's aggressive approach. It helped define reality for me.

Learning from Mark Driscoll led me to John Piper. Under these teachers was the first time I was introduced to Calvinism as a theological philosophy. This is theology made popular by reformer John Calvin. Followers of Calvin teach the acronym TULIP for understanding the Christian story. TULIP stands for:

> *Total depravity*: Because of our sinfulness, we are as good as dead. We cannot choose to be undead to our sin any more than a literal corpse could wish to be brought back to life. Even if told how to find life, we are unable to give ourselves life. For those of us destined for hell, our time on earth is as good as we are ever going to get. (Later, when I deconstructed, this construct felt especially pernicious when considering my friend Jack.)
>
> *Unconditional Election*: Only God has the agency to save humanity from the wrath he will unleash on our sin, we cannot ask for it. God, in his sovereignty, chooses some to save, and chooses the majority to torment forever in hell. We cannot choose to be saved, we cannot choose to be unsaved. We are unconditionally elected.
>
> *Limited Atonement*: Christ's work of atonement was limited only for the remnant God chooses to save. He did not die for everyone.
>
> *Irresistible Grace*: If God gives grace to you, there is nothing in the world you can do to thwart it, or to prevent God from taking you to heaven.
>
> *Preservation of the Saints*: Once you are saved, even if you're living like the Devil, you are always saved.

In addition to this, I embraced their theology of God's complete and utter sovereignty. Everything that occurs happens because God wills it. When we sin, it's because God predetermined we would sin. When an orphanage is built or a hospital constructed in a third-world country, God, in his goodness, predetermined that people would build those things. In the same way, if a man takes a gun into an elementary school and slaughters twenty six-and seven-year-old kids, as well as six adult staff, God also predetermined that would occur. And when we ask God why bad things like this happen we are asking the wrong question. Why does God allow anything other than tragedy to occur? We are so sinful and vile, we don't deserve better treatment. The most important endgame God has is to bring himself glory. God is glorified when he makes people build homeless shelters and God is glorified when genocide is committed in Rwanda. When God acts it is to give himself glory.

(I'm aware this is an overly simplistic explanation of reformed theology, for more on it and its pitfalls check out the excellent book *Young, Restless, and No Longer Reformed* by Austin Fischer.)

This is theology I once believed and taught. And millions of people are taught this, believe it, and defend it. Suffice it to say that the more I ventured into what is called reformed theology, the less gracious I became toward others and to myself. In his book, *The God Delusion*, scientist and professor Richard Dawkins says this about God:

> The God of the Bible is arguably the most unpleasant character in all fiction: jealous and proud of it; a petty, unjust, unforgiving control-freak; a vindictive, bloodthirsty ethnic cleanser; a misogynistic, homophobic, racist, infanticidal, genocidal, filicidal, pestilential, megalomaniacal, sadomasochistic, capriciously malevolent bully.

As a side note, can I suggest if you're interested in atheist philosophy, steer clear of folks like Richard Dawkins? Might I suggest Friedrich Nietzsche? Dawkins has a comically nonacademic approach to Scripture and church history. He has built his career critiquing a very small, oftentimes uninformed, puddle in the massive pool of historic Christianity. He's not a very compelling or well-rounded atheist. However, when I think back about my time with TULIP fever, retrospect shows this quote is not that far off from how I perceived God.

Speaking of predestination and predeterminism, as a closeted person, these theologies absolutely mortified me. I never chose to feel the way I did, I never asked for it. This theology meant God gave me those things. And seeing as I was convinced of the evils in my hidden desires, I couldn't shake the feeling I was not one of God's elect. It felt plausible to believe God created me just to curse me with desires I did not want, and to torment me forever in hell. I decided my only hope was to live as righteously as I could, and maybe that would prove to myself I was indeed one of God's elect. I just had to prove I was good enough. I wasn't acceptable, so I had to make myself acceptable. This meant getting more hard-lined, rigid, and graceless about my beliefs than ever.

Around this time a book came out called *Love Wins*. Where the author, Rob Bell, called into to question the ways some Christians have been talking about hell since the 1500s. Before I even knew what the book was about Mark Driscoll, John Piper, Franklin Graham Jr., and many others led a witch hunt against it. The reaction to it was so swift I don't think most of the people rioting against it even had enough time to read it. Overnight, it seemed as if the name Rob Bell had become a cuss word in my circles. This instilled in me the idea of theology being a war of ideologies. There were good guys (of course the folks I listened to were the good guys) and there were bad guys. Our circles labeled Rob Bell and his fellow heretics as the Emergent Church. The Emergent Church may have seemed trendy and laid back, but they were wolves in sheep's clothing as far as I was concerned. I even read a book with a group from church called *Why We're Not Emergent*. I didn't want to take the time to hear these people out and decide for myself what I thought of it, I wanted to be told how to think about this. I didn't want to grow or learn, I wanted ammo for the fight against the heretical progressives.

In time, I would tone down the way I presented my disapproval of these people and their views, but I still held strong to my convictions. I just got tired of being a jerk all the time. I approached life and faith with 100 percent certainty, until Mother's Day, May 13th, 2012.

CHAPTER SIX

Remember You Like Yesterday

"Give sorrow words; the grief that does not speak knits up the over wrought heart and bids it break."
—WILLIAM SHAKESPEARE

"Be gracious to me, O Lord, for I am in distress, my eye wastes away from grief, my soul and body also."
—PSALM 31:9 (NRSV)

I FEEL LIKE I can't breathe, but I am in too much shock to be bothered by it. I don't say anything. I can only see my dad's face. He had been crying, and he didn't want to have this talk. He thought things would end differently. The room is cold, although it probably isn't actually cold because it is the middle of May. Still, I feel cold. Colder than I ever have. I sit on our recliner. A moment frozen in time. I want to cry but I can't. After a few moments, I finally say:

"I wasn't expecting this . . . I was counting on things turning around."

Twenty minutes ago, I was sitting in a theater watching *The Hunger Games* for the fourth time with Jordan. I was eating popcorn and I was sad Rue just met her end. I checked my phone and noticed I had twelve missed calls from my dad. My dad never calls that many times. I run out of the theater and into the hallway, knowing in the pit of my stomach why he called that many times. I call my dad back.

"Tony, where are you?" are his first words.

"I'm at the movies. Why did you call me so many times?"

PART I: BEAUTIFUL FAITH SHACKLED IN SHAME

"You need to come home right now," he responds abruptly.

"Is it Mom?" I respond. There is a brief pause on his end.

"Just come home."

I run back into the theater to tell Jordan I need to get home ASAP. We rush out of the building and into my little black Chevy Cavalier. I drive home as quickly as I can, going ten to fifteen miles an hour over the speed limit.

Now I'm sitting on the recliner my mom spent many evenings on during her OxyContin-induced hazes.

"How did it happen?" I ask my dad.

"We won't know for sure until they do an autopsy, but she probably overdosed."

"Of course, she did," I reply, glaring at the floor.

Guilt begins to shower over me as a thought I want to keep at bay breaks through the barriers of my mind: this is my fault.

You see, today is Mother's Day. I purposely did not reach out to her. I made my own defiant statement that she would have to sober up before I'd celebrate her as my mom again. I haven't spoken to my mother in a month. In fact, the last time I spoke with her was Easter Sunday. She came to church high as a kite, and made inappropriate comments to one of my students. I drove her home and told her I did not want to see her anymore. Ten months before this she left my dad for a creep who kicked her out after he got her disability check, she lived on the streets and then was living in a worn-down apartment, she ceased being the woman I knew. She came to church the week after our confrontation, and I hid from her. I stayed at opposite sides of the room from her, and when she would walk toward me I would leave, pretending not to see her.

Those were my last interactions with my mom. The woman who taught me about the world-changing love of Jesus, my paragon of nurturing love. My last moments with her were spent telling her I didn't want to see her again, and avoiding her as she tried to connect with me.

These thoughts take over my mind. I finally start crying. *It's my fault*, I repeat over and over in my mind. I refuse to say it out loud because I don't want to hear my dad try to correct me. My mind is made up and I don't want to argue with him.

Jordan is waiting outside as my dad delivers the news to me. You could wait a million lifetimes and never find a friend as good as him. I go outside and tell him what happened. After a hug and some tears, he asks me what I need, and if he wants me to call our people. I say yes.

A half hour later I am sitting with my closest friends around a table. We cry, we hug, we mourn. We go out for milkshakes, because what else are you supposed to do on the worst day of your life? None of us really know what to say, but that doesn't matter, what matters is they are here. As I sit at the table in the diner, my friends carry on conversation with each other. They talk about their days, tell funny stories, and they laugh. I laugh too. But I can't help but notice my laughs are forced and empty. I am not able to join in sincerely. I'm not able to shake the growing, dreaded reality that I am now a son without a mom, and nothing will change that. I realize my life will never be the same, and because of how she went, I will fight this dread for years and years to come.

After my friends leave, Dennis agrees to stay the night. He falls asleep on my bedroom floor, and I sit in the living room attempting to process what is happening. I take out my phone, and call my mom just to listen to her voice on her voicemail. I know that soon her phone will be disconnected, and I don't know if we have any home videos. This will be my last time getting to hear her voice.

> There is no way to prepare for the impact of grief. It is like your soul has been demolished by a freight train.

So, I call her again, and again. I beg God for her to answer and have all this be a big misunderstanding. But she does not answer. She will never answer again.

I can't believe it. I prayed for years for her to get sober. I fasted for weeks. My friends prayed for her. My church and family prayed for her. I begged her to get clean. The possibility of her dying wasn't even on my radar. I was full of faith God would heal her and she would make a turn around. That didn't happen.

I don't understand why he answers some prayers and ignores others. I used to think he said no because there was a better yes coming, but not this time. When it comes to saving my mom or letting her die, there is no better answer than yes to saving her. There is no way to prepare for the impact of grief. It is like your soul has been demolished by a freight train. I pray and beg for God to offer a little grace. I ask him to get me through this. And while I don't know it at the time, he will come through on that prayer.

CHAPTER SEVEN

The Twists in My Story

> "To be fully seen by somebody, and to be loved anyhow-this is a human offering that can border on miraculous."
> —ELIZABETH GILBERT

> "Live happily with the woman you love through all the meaningless days God has given you under the sun."
> —ECCLESIASTES 9:9 (NIV)

What is Happening to Me?

I TOOK VERY LITTLE time off of work after my mother's death. I believed I needed to power through and couldn't afford to stop and process for too long. This has led to much of the dysfunction I still experience today. Too much time spent alone processing her death only seemed to lead me toward a nagging doubt about whether or not God cared at all for his creation. I still read my Bible, fought to hang onto my beliefs, prayed, and moved forward as much as I could for as long as I could without confronting those doubts.

Two months after my mom's death my buddy introduced me to this girl he was interested in. Her name was Kelsey, and to be totally honest, I didn't think much of her. This friend was always looking for "the one" and I figured she was just another "one" who eventually would disappear. We hung out as a group a few times, and then eventually she ended things with him.

However, she and I kept spending time together with some of our other friends. We started texting more frequently when we weren't together. Slowly I began to notice how wonderful she was. She had a snarky spark in her that captivated me, but she was also sweet and empathetic. I started feeling something in my gut that I didn't know what to do with. I would get nervous whenever I was around her. I put pressure on myself to appear suave (with comically low results) whenever I knew I was going to see her.

I was apprehensive to jump to the conclusion that I had romantic feelings for her. In the past whenever I felt a connection with a girl I rushed as fast as I could into a relationship only to realize I didn't actually care for them in a romantic way, as much as I wanted to. I hurt some good people with my behavior and I did not want to do that again. So, I waited. I kept spending time with her. Whenever I wasn't with her I couldn't wait to be with her again. I didn't know what sort of magic this Kelsey girl had that made me feel these things for her, but it was working.

The Girl of My Dreams

The following Mother's Day, the first one without my mom, was filled with tears of a different kind. Kelsey and I had been spending time together for almost a year at this point. We both had Tuesday mornings off, so we cultivated a ritual of breakfast together every Tuesday. We took turns reading *The Great Divorce* to each other and watched movies. And there was no denying this girl had totally captured my heart. I celebrated Mother's Day with a friend and his family. After lunch, he and I sat on his back deck and talked. He made note of the fact that Kelsey and I had been spending so much time together, and asked me if I liked her, you know, "in that way." I said yes. And in that moment, I was so overcome with emotion that tears filled my eyes.

> This was a girl I could only dream of. Beautiful, hilarious, self-aware, talented, and the sweetest person you were ever likely to meet.

"I've never felt this way before. I never thought I would ever feel this way," I told him.

This was a girl I could only dream of. Beautiful, hilarious, self-aware, talented, and the sweetest person you were ever likely to meet. I was falling hard for her, and I could sense, even then, she was going to be my partner for the rest of my life. The joy of that thought brought tears to my eyes. It still does.

Wait, What?

I know what some of you are thinking, "I thought this dude was gay? What's this girl of my dreams plot twist?"

Crazy, right? I call Kelsey the girl of my dreams because I never thought in my wildest dreams I would feel this way about anyone. I prayed for years and years for a girl like her to come along, and then she did. In fact, I feel toward her more love than I knew was possible to experience. However, I am not so ignorant as to think that people who identify as gay or lesbian are going to fall in love with the opposite sex if they just pray for it long enough. Many have believed this promise at the expensive of taking severe blows to their mental health. I'm not convinced this happened because I "prayed the gay away."

Promising people this has led countless LGBTQ+ folks to places of deep shame, depression, and in many cases, suicide. I married this girl. I love this woman more than the air I breath, but my struggles with my sexuality did not change.

Kelsey is an answer to my prayers. Prayers for companionship, love, a family, a partner. She is the answer to all those prayers and more. There are not a lot of areas in my life I can look at and say, "God has definitely heard me." But this is one of them. He promised me a life that was thrilling and fulfilling, and Kelsey is the biggest, most important piece to that puzzle.

The Best and Worst

We were engaged on St. Patrick's Day, 2014. I learned to play the song "Pistol" by Dustin Kensrue on guitar, and sang to her. Afterward I got on one knee and popped the question. We celebrated with our friends, and began planning the wedding. I was overjoyed . . . the girl of my dreams said *yes*. However, in the months leading up to our wedding something began to take place in me. A deep fear started growing. I knew if Kelsey and I were going to stand a chance at doing marriage well I would have to tell her my story, my whole story. I knew this but refused to do it. Even still there was a thought that scared me more than coming out to her: What if after getting married I realized I really was just gay? What if I marry her and break her heart? What if I fall in love with a man, as I felt I had a few times in the past? Looking back now I realize these are thoughts any rational person could have before they get married, regardless of the gender of the person they are marrying. Remember though, I was Mr. Five-Point Calvinist who loved an extra heaping of shame with his secrets. I was fighting the nagging thought in the back of my head that no matter how hard I tried to do and be good, I was created by God to be a reprobate.

I forced myself to suppress those fears and we moved forward. We were married on December 13th, 2014 (that's 12/13/14 for those paying attention). We had a beautiful ceremony, and as I write this it remains the best day of my life. We were surrounded by our church, family, and friends. We worshipped loudly, prayed deeply, laughed heartily. My spiritual father and pastor performed our wedding, and I had both Dennis and Jordan as my best men. We went to Disneyland for our honeymoon and came back to a little apartment as our first home.

It didn't take long after we got married for me to realize how my secrets affected our relationship. She gave everything she had to our marriage, and all I had to offer in return was my hiding. No matter how hard I tried I couldn't make our marriage feel genuine. The more I hid from her, the more the fears of self-sabotage pervaded my mind. This sparked a torment I would continually experience over the next couple months. Panic attacks and breakdowns at least once a week. Every thought and feeling that flowed in me was rooted in fear and shame. And for the first time since high school, I again wanted to die. Whenever people asked me why I thought this was happening so frequently, I responded with my favorite excuse: *I don't know.* But I knew. I was married to the most outstanding person I had ever met, I couldn't let her in, and I feared if I didn't learn to do it I was going to lose her.

I couldn't take it anymore. One evening a group of us from church went to watch *Avengers: Age of Ultron* (the weakest *Avengers* movie by the way). After the movie, I asked Dennis to come over and talk. I feared what would happen to me if I didn't tell somebody, and I couldn't tell Kelsey. We were raised to believe same-sex attraction was a chosen path of sin. I could not risk her leaving me, but I needed to tell somebody, if only to allow myself the opportunity to breath. So, that Thursday night Dennis and I stood under the carport of my apartment. He leaned against my car with his hands in his pockets and a concerned look on his face as I fumbled my way through my story. I explained everything to him: the secret I had been keeping my whole life, the fears I had that I would sabotage my marriage, that even at one point in our own friendship I thought I was in love with him. Everything. He handled it better than I could have hoped. He affirmed me, told me he loved me, hugged me. He didn't seem afraid of me, he still talked to and looked at me like I was, well, me.

I felt a little better after our conversation. The panic attacks and the depression lessoned significantly. But Dennis knew I was not well. He saw me headed down a destructive path and didn't know what to do. He told someone in the church that had sworn confidentiality to him. He went looking for advice on how to help me. This person was on staff with the church I worked at, and had also seen unhealthy patterns in me. In what I now know to be an attempt to help me this person went to my lead pastor and told him everything. And in an instant the world began to crumble. The best season of my life, a season of repairing my broken heart from my mom, living out my dream of doing ministry, falling in love, and getting married, quickly gave way to one of the worst.

Laid Bare before the City

There's a fascinating little book in the Old Testament called Hosea. Hosea was a prophet for the nation of Israel. In the Scriptures the prophetic calling was a holy and sometimes distinguished office. Well, one day God tells Hosea to marry a woman named Gomer (Gomer? That's strike one, God.), and Gomer was a prostitute (strike two). Hosea marries her, and has three children with the woman. Eventually this woman again returns to her former profession, and leaves Hosea and their family. God tells Hosea to go find her and buy her back, and Hosea does as he is commanded despite the shame and humiliation it would bring him. Even though his wife returned to a life of prostitution, and even though her name was Gomer, Hosea obeyed. God is using Hosea's life to make a point: God is like Hosea, Israel is like Gomer. God is committed to Israel like a faithful husband even though Israel continually abandons the everlasting love of God for other gods (other lovers). And even though Israel does this over and over again, God still pursues Israel with his love, even going to the point of shaming himself in seeking Israel out. It's a powerful story about the unconditional love of God and the human propensity to reject that love.

Here's what stands out to me about this story: Gomer, being a prostitute, would have been selling herself in the public parts of the city. It was the only place she could have drummed up business. So, here's this holy prophet of God in front of the whole city, in the seedy parts of town, looking for a prostitute. I don't think I need to tell you that in this time the shame of taking back an adulteress wife, let alone *buying* one back, was unimaginable. And yet there Hosea was, buying back his wife, with his shame laid bare before the city. A public disgrace.

For anyone who works a job that requires a fair amount of work with the public, when they are removed from that assignment for reasons deemed by the community as disqualifying, they experience a similar form of public disgrace. They too are laid bare before their community. It's the price people pay for living life in the public arena. It's also why people with larger platforms so often crumble under the weight of that pressure.

My pastor handled the situation as well as he could have. He let me know that for the foreseeable future I would no longer be able to do ministry at that church. He made it very clear this was not a punitive decision, rather one he hoped would see my life and marriage brought to a place of health. He told me he loved me, and that he wanted me to stay at that church and get well. He paid for Kelsey and I to get away and connect as I would be giving her some pretty big news. He had questions about my sexuality, about whether or not I had an affair with one of our volunteer leaders, if I wanted to get healthy and stay married to Kelsey. I answered the questions: I've felt this way as long as I can remember, I would never cheat on my wife, and of course I want to get healthy and stay married. So, after five years on staff at the church, I was asked to step down.

I went home and broke the news to Kelsey. I told her everything. It was a lot to take in, and no matter how much I tried to tell her I only loved her, everything she thought she knew about me was brought into question. There was dishonesty on my part, and fear on her part. Fear that I wanted to be with a man more than I wanted to be with her. And remember, we believed that experiencing attraction to the same sex was a chosen path of abominable sin. How could she accept that I loved her and chose her, when I was also "choosing" this other path? In order for us to move forward, this poorly constructed and intellectually narrow idea had to crumble.

Things felt broken very early on in our marriage. We told her family everything, we told my family everything, and a few of our closest friends. In just a few days more people knew my secret than I ever wanted to know. But it was good. Mostly, I was still loved and accepted. My dad took the news incredibly well, and I realized I could have told him as soon as I knew about it.

Kelsey and I were determined to make things work. We did a lot of counseling. Each of us on our own, and then together. We learned more about each other in our first year of marriage than most couples do in their first five. It was hard, but over time we began to heal together. She learned to trust me and I learned to stop hiding. And, even though we haven't been married for very long, I am happy to say we have had each other's backs every step of the way since then. Even when everything around has gone to chaos, we have stayed unified.

Outted

Even though things between Kelsey and I were being put back together, it didn't prevent me from feeling like everything else had fallen apart. I spent the majority of my life in partial hiding, never allowing anyone to see the true me. So, to suddenly have to tell as many people as I did, as quickly as I did, was both liberating and invasive. To be seen, known, and still accepted is liberating. To have the pieces of yourself you have nearly died to keep hidden suddenly exposed to the people who know you best, before you're ready to tell them, is invasive. Not to mention, I was no longer in ministry. I never even thought this could be true of me, but I had no sense of self outside of my role in ministry. I got saved when I was sixteen and immediately led a Bible study for my peers on campus, and had not stopped doing ministry since then. One of my most defining features was lost, and I had to rediscover who I was—not as a youth pastor, not as a preacher, not as a disciple of my pastor, but as Tony, a follower of Jesus.

Finding my place in church instantly became the most difficult transition out of this whole ordeal. My pastor made the choice not to tell the church as to why I was stepping down, only to say we were being given space to work on our marriage, which was appreciated. However, it would not be long before people started coming up to me at church asking about a rumor they heard about me being gay. I started receiving text messages, social media messages, emails, and phone calls from a variety of different people from the church inquiring about rumors they had heard about why I stepped down. The most common one was I had been having an affair with a man. Many people whom neither I nor Kelsey told the secret to knew the secret. Over and over again I had to correct the rumors with the truth.

More often than not the truth was met with compassion, but not always. One parent of a student formerly in my middle school group point-blank asked me if I had "done anything inappropriate" with their child. "I trusted my son with you. Did anything happen between you two?" they asked me. For this person, the leap between being LGBTQ+ and being a pedophile was short. They told me of an article they read which broke down how homosexuality was a depraved and slippery slope into pedophilia—a destructive misconception not uncommon in some church circles to this day. For the record, straight men are astronomically more likely to be found guilty of pedophilia than gay men.

I don't know who shared my story without my permission. Some close friend, family member, staff member, or elder at the church told the wrong person, and soon many people were coming up with their own versions of my story. It doesn't matter who said it. With my secret out I always felt on guard, fearing I would be met with rejection or accusations of unspeakable evil. I started losing the bright and fulfilling love for church I once had.

The difficulties only began to pile up. I did not know how to be at church without also helping to run the place. People who once treated me with love and respect would no longer give me the time of day. Now I don't know that it was because they were homophobic, but in the state of mind I was in it sure felt like it. Anxiety and depression began to dictate the majority of my decisions. We would take weeks, sometimes over a month off from church. If I was five minutes late to a service when I was on staff, even if I didn't have any responsibilities that morning, my phone would be ringing off the hook with people wondering where I was. But now that I wasn't leading, Kelsey and I could miss six weeks in a row without so much as a text message. This isn't to make Kelsey and I out to be victims or say the church was bad. I still, to this day, love that church deeply. What was happening to us was nothing I had not done to many people myself. People stop showing up and unless they're right in front of you sometimes you just don't notice they aren't there. Still, at the time, we took it as a heavy blow.

During this season of my life I felt as though my spiritual home and life were slowly slipping away. Before, on any given Sunday I would be met with big hugs and genuine smiles in our church atrium, but after stepping down and addressing so many rumors, I felt as though I were a stranger in someone else's house. Whereas at one point I could sit in our sanctuary and be moved to tears by the presence of God, I now sat in the pews with no sense of any Divine Being, just a looming emptiness inside my heart. Before I would sometimes stay over an hour after our service playing games with our students and talking with parents; I was now home within ten minutes of the service ending. The church hadn't changed, I had. Try as I might to engage with people and the Spirit in the ways I had before, I couldn't shake the feeling I was running on empty. I didn't want to lose my sense of connection with church and with God, but I was. It was slipping away quickly.

CHAPTER EIGHT

Slippery Slope

"Why is it so cruelly inconceivable to comprehend God with the senses? Why does he hide in a cloud of half promises and unseen miracles? How can we believe in the faithful when we lack faith? What will happen to us who want to believe, but cannot? What about those who neither want nor can believe? Why can't I kill God in me? Why does he live on in me in a humiliating way—despite my wanting to rip Him from my heart? Why is he, despite all, a mocking reality I can't be rid of?"

—THE SEVENTH SEAL (1957)

"My God, my God, why have you forsaken me? Why are you so far away from saving me, so far away from my cries of anguish?"

—PSALM 22:1 (NIV)

Falling into Mystery

AS I STRUGGLED TO adapt to civilian life in my church something unexpected happened: as I have expressed before, I had plenty of questions for God surrounding my mother's death, but I had never heard the Christians I respected wrestle with those specific and terrifying questions. In the past, whenever I heard someone ask these questions it sounded like some Rob Bell heresy to me. So, I hid them. Rather than confront my inquiries and doubts, I tried to keep them as hidden as my sexuality. Yet with the

PART I: BEAUTIFUL FAITH SHACKLED IN SHAME

life-giving energy I once received from church withering away, I lost the ability to keep my questions in check. I was terrified. I was standing on the edge of a cliff and could not see anything more than fog and mist below. The wind was blowing hard, and I was losing my balance. At the edge of certainty, I was about to fall into mystery.

I noticed something in my thinking changed after losing my position. There wasn't as many people paying attention to me anymore. I had questions I was holding back because I did not want to be perceived as unfaithful or heretical. Well, now I had no reason to hide. I knew my intention wasn't to be in defiance of God or to be dishonorable. I knew I wasn't being hubristic by struggling with doubt. I also knew unless I started addressing the cognitive dissonance I was experiencing I was going to go crazy. So, I took the plunge and dove headfirst into the mystery.

Why did God let my mom die? Did God create my mom a reprobate? Was she in hell, burning forever? My mother died because of how much opioids she had pumped into her system. Surely, she was not one of God's elect. Did God, in his sovereignty, cause my mom to fall deeper and deeper into her addiction until it claimed her life? Why would God do that? Well, my reformed thinking would tell me he did it for his glory, because God does everything for his own glory. My next question was: Why would that bring God glory? What kind of God is glorified by a wife and mother of two dying of a drug overdose, especially when so much time had been spent begging him to rescue her?

I came to a realization that I wanted nothing to do with the God responsible for my mother's death. That God was directly responsible for the suffering of my mother (and every other person who has ever suffered and died), and could not be called good. Not by any discernable metric could this God be considered loving, or merciful, or good.

So, I had three options at this point: 1) I could spend the rest of my life hating this God; 2) I could abandon faith in God all together; or 3) I could lean further into my questions and potentially discover a God who was different from who I thought he was. Was God the same God my mother introduced me to all those years ago, who revealed himself to me through the revelation of love? Or was that merely a vivid fairytale? Or maybe God was actually this Being who arbitrarily chooses some to heal and others to die, some to save and others to kill, some destined for paradise and others to torture forever in hell.

I didn't know where this journey was going to take me, but I had started my free-fall into mystery, and there was no turning back.

The Jesus Who Gets You in Trouble

Around this time, I started reading books about God from perspectives I would have never considered before. I read over a hundred books over the next two years, all addressing different perspectives and interpretations of the Christian story. For some people, a hundred books in two years is nothing, but it was a lot for me. Also, some of them may have been audio books. I can't remember how I stumbled upon most of these books. They all seemed to find me, and that was a piece of grace from God. Who knows where I would be now if I had to travel the road of deconstruction without these authorial pastors and coaches to help me along the way? This is why I am so convinced one of the healthiest and most beneficial disciplines a person can have is regular reading.

The first major formational book for me was *Fight: A Christian Case for Nonviolence* by Preston Sprinkle. This book felt like a new exposure to Jesus. Not the American, conservative evangelical, gun-wielding, white Jesus who spoke in platitudes and served as an attractive mascot for my nationalistic and reformed tendencies, but *Jesus*, the ancient near Eastern, nonviolent revolutionary. Rather than be used as a puppet of the government this Jesus exposed the evils of empire by ushering in a new, upside-down empire of his own (more on this later). Preston showed me this Jesus lived in defiance of the cultural customs and norms of his time, and revealed a deeper, truer power than financial and military might. Jesus came to show us a new way to be human. But this new humanity was not simply one of asceticism and abstinence from certain sins, but one of beauty, justice, and action. Living this new Jesus Way meant taking a step away from the empires and governments of this world, and taking a step toward the new kingdom God was bringing here and now, through our allegiance to Jesus. The Jesus Preston was writing about was so much more compelling, challenging, and risky than the Jesus I had read and taught about up to that point. Before, I'm sorry to say, Jesus was only useful to me for his atoning work on the cross. I had looked at his words and deeds as helpful little life lessons, but did not consider them practical when the rubber met the road. On the contrary, the teachings of Christ were far from little life lessons. Jesus' words are a treatise for citizens of the kingdom of heaven, and they matter most when it's most inconvenient to live them out.

Not only that, the book was rooted in a hope for resurrection. Resurrection could make all the lofty, confusing, scary things Jesus taught us to do possible, even loving your enemies. You can truly lose your life to the mission of the kingdom because the story God is writing for us ends in resurrection. You can even lose your life to love your enemies because resurrection is the new reality for Christians. Resurrection reality means society may view you as a foolish failure, but you are actually accomplishing the greatest good there is in life. In the book, Preston writes:

> Viewed from one angle, Jesus' entire ministry of peace was a colossal failure. But the resurrection changed everything for Him. And the resurrection changed everything for us. We no longer view the world through the dim mist of justice and reward, but through the bright lens of resurrection, where suffering leads to glory and slaughtered lambs rule the earth.

Another book that got me thinking more seriously about Jesus early on was *The Irresistible Revolution* by Shane Claiborne. Shane introduced me to a Jesus who "comforts the disturbed and disturbs the comfortable." In this work, he seriously considers questions I had never been forced to confront (outside of *Fight*): What if Jesus actually meant the things he said, and what if he actually expects us to follow suit? What if Jesus really meant it when he told us to love our enemies, give to the poor, welcome the stranger? What if we were really meant to live recklessly generous lives? What if we were meant to love our neighbors and enemies just as much as we loved ourselves? What if the Jesus I had been preaching and reading about was tainted by a lens of American exceptionalism and consumerist culture? What if Jesus isn't pleased with churches spending millions of dollars on buildings and remodels while, according to the UN website, twenty five thousand people die every day from starvation? What if Christians were meant to be better known for their ability to restore communities, heal brokenness, and feed the hungry than they were for their concert hall-style buildings? What if the name-it-and-claim-it message taught by so many is actually a defamation of the true Christ of Scripture and tradition?

These books had given me a lot to think about, and I learned these observations were not always appreciated by some of the churchfolk I knew. These new ways of seeing Jesus began to enliven something I felt was fading in me. I was excited to talk about this Jesus who was reclaiming my heart.

So, I started having coffee with different friends who were Christians, and I shared with them the new things I was learning. The responses I got ranged from sympathetic ("Yes, this makes a lot of sense. But it's not how things are done") to the moderate ("It just isn't practical, enemy love and radical generosity") to the frustrated ("money given to churches is God's money and God can do with it what he pleases. If he wants to build big buildings who are we to stop him?"). With each talk, even the more positive ones, I walked away more discouraged, and as my discouragement grew, my anger grew toward church as a whole. The radical mission of Christ seemed clear, but the waters were being muddied.

Now I understand my anger may have been misplaced (as is often the case with me). This way of talking about Jesus was new, uncomfortable, and, well, disturbing. People don't react well when they're disturbed. I was falling in love with a clearer picture of Jesus than I ever had before, but few around me found following this Jesus very realistic. Was this the narrow road Jesus spoke of in Matthew 7, the one only few will find? Was finding this Jesus Way totally unrealistic what he meant when he repeatedly said, "Oh you of little faith?" (Matt 8:26 NIV). Or, the scariest option, maybe my friends were right. Maybe it was unrealistic. But if I couldn't take what Jesus had to say seriously, why should I take any of the Bible seriously? If Jesus is God, it seems like this whole thing should hinge on whether or not what he was saying should be followed. Maybe there was no Jesus, not a Divine one anyway. The thought scared me, but I moved forward.

Two other books that were formative to me during this time were *Water to Wine* by Brian Zahnd and *Generous Orthodoxy* by Brian McLaren. In *Water to Wine*, Zahnd talked about faith transitions and faithfully following your new revelations of Jesus. He spoke about life with God as if it were a progressing revelation. We never really get it all figured out, and we must hold our dogmas with open hands because we are often wrong in our interpretations, and wrong in the motives behind our interpretations. If we aren't changing our minds from time to time we aren't growing, and if we aren't growing we aren't really listening to the Spirit. God is taking us on a journey of mystery and discovery. A growing faith means it moves, changes, and evolves: like water to wine. And, rather than fearing or condemning this reality, Zahnd embraced it. He gave me the pastoral permission I needed to keep following where my questions were leading me. The God Zahnd was writing about wasn't easily angered or intimidated by our questions, he even seemed to welcome them. The way Zahnd wrote about

PART I: BEAUTIFUL FAITH SHACKLED IN SHAME

God gave me the sense it was possibly the Spirit leading me to these new places.

Reading *Generous Orthodoxy* felt like a sneaky and joyfully rebellious thing to do. Remember that book I mentioned reading a few years prior called *Why We're Not Emergent, By Two Guys Who Should Be*? That book tore apart Brian McLaren, making him out to be a false prophet of sorts, a wolf in sheep's clothing, a more dangerous Rob Bell. But the subtitle for *Generous Orthodoxy* was: "Why I am a missional, evangelical, post/protestant, liberal/conservative, mystical/poetic, biblical, charismatic/contemplative, fundamentalist/Calvinist, Anabaptist/Anglican, Methodist, catholic, green, incarnational, depressed-yet hopeful, emergent, unfinished Christian." How was I *not* supposed to read this? It seemed primed for the season of life I was in. And it was. Brian pointed out the charismatic/reformed tradition I came from was merely one of many Christian traditions all around the world. Not only that, but this tradition was one of the younger expressions of Christianity. For me church history started at the dawn of the Reformation in 1517. These other expressions of Christianity I had once dismissed as unbiblical or heretical actually had a longer expression of faith than the one I was brought up in. I realized my way of interpreting Christ and Scripture was mostly influenced by thinkers and preachers from 500 years ago, and I had ignored the 1,500 years of tradition and theology before that. Who was I to say that ancient Christians didn't actually love God as much as those of us who followed in the footsteps of Martin Luther and John Calvin? I learned a fancy word during this time—*hermeneutic*. Hermeneutic is an interpretive lens applied to exemplary texts, namely Scripture.

I had never before realized that my hermeneutic for Scripture was not only one of many, but not even the oldest or most orthodox one out there! I lived and died on the idea of the Bible being read as the infallible, error-free, plenary, final revelation from God, and it should be read as literally as possible as frequently as possible. To read it in any other way was to deny the Bible's authority, and deny God himself. The realization that this lens really only gained traction during the Enlightenment period in the eighteenth century, and that it isn't even the oldest way of reading Scripture, messed with my categories. Shoot, learning there was more than one way of reading Scripture at all messed me up. Before, anyone who asserted an alternative hermeneutic was easy to dismiss as a new-age heretic who only wanted to make Scripture more palatable. But now I was confronted with my own hubris. Could I really say that I and my tribe had found the *only way* to read the Bible, and the majority of other Christians throughout history were heretics at worst and deeply naïve at best? I was stunned to realize I didn't actually believe in the Bible's authority, I believed in the authority of the people who taught me to read the Bible. I did not place the authority on Scripture, I placed it on my interpretive lens, and there is a difference.

Was the way I had been reading the Bible faithful to the authorial intent of the text? Was my literalist, infallible hermeneutic trying to fit the Bible into categories it was never meant to fit into? What was the right way of reading the Bible, then? What does this mean about the reliability of Jesus, or the afterlife, or the resurrection? What does this mean about the sins it speaks of, like queer romance? As if I didn't have enough questions. Not only did I have to find a new way of relating to God, but I had to find out which way I was meant to read the Bible. All the while the creeping doubt in my mind was whispering there was no right way to read the Bible. Maybe it was just an ancient fairytale book with no more authority on spirituality and history than Homer's *Iliad*.

I think at this point it is important to point out this is not to say that historic Christians did not find the Bible to be inspired by God. Christians have always believed, for the most part, the Bible is uniquely authoritative and revelatory to the faith. However, this does not mean Christians have always found the best way of reading the Bible was to read it as literally as possible, nor does it mean early Christians insisted it was free of errors (by error I mean contradicting accounts or accounts blatantly refuted by science or history). More on this later.

Needless to say, discussing these new discoveries with some of my church friends did not go over very well. So, I did the next best thing I could do (he writes sarcastically): I took the discussion to Facebook. Let me say now I think social media is a terrible platform for debating heated topics. Any forum where the persons voice, facial expressions, and mannerisms cannot be taken in is a horrendous place to talk about sensitive issues. Social media was an alluring venue for people like me, who longed for their voice to be heard. So, just about every new thought and idea I had was posted to Facebook. Add to that the fact I'm not very good at steering away from confrontation, and I grew quite the reputation for being a Facebook antagonist. It was poor choices on my part, and I get to shake my head in shame every day when I check my Facebook Memories.

PART I: BEAUTIFUL FAITH SHACKLED IN SHAME

A Hard Goodbye

Taking the time to seriously consider ideas I had previously found offensive only added to my insecurities at church. I was not aware of there being much of a range of thought when it came to how we read the Bible or calling into question whether or not Jesus was condoning of affluent American idealism in the church. Between feeling as though the secret of my sexuality had spread throughout the church, and knowing I was publicly asking questions that curated anger with a few people in my community, I felt more like a pariah each week. I was faced with a choice. I knew I could not continue on the path I was on and stay in my church without breeding divisive contention. I wanted to discuss and wrestle with these things without feeling like I was being pressed into coming to conclusions I wasn't ready to arrive at. But doing this came at a high price: a deep sense of separation between me and the community that raised me. Where the folks around me saw black-and-white simple answers, I only saw grey.

I could try to stop confronting these things and go back to who I was. I could try to pretend these questions weren't compelling, to read the Bible the same way I always had, and I did try, but whenever I did, I felt God slipping further and further away from me. You see, the folks around me seemed to think my doubt and angst was a result of the questions and tensions I was leaning into. But the opposite was true. In fact, during this season I only ever felt a sense that God was real when I was diving into the mystery. They were right about one thing, however: doubt was replacing faith in my heart. The more I read, the more questions I had. The more questions I had, the less certainty I had. Even if learning about nonviolence and radical love evoked warmth in my heart, it was a warmth that flickered briefly in the deep, cold, fog of doubt within. The paradox here was if I stopped reading, stopped learning, if I tried to rely on my old habits of devotion, I felt an existential dread I was utterly unfamiliar with, but to keep searching was to continue to find holes in what I thought was an air-tight belief system. There was no winning.

Kelsey, Dennis, myself, and a few others had started a home group, totally separate from our church, to be a place people could come and discuss the new things they were learning. A place for people to confront their doubts, confess their shame, learn new things, and try to find God; all within a safe, open, judgment-free environment. This was concerning to some people from our church, who had at first heard that we were treating it like a church plant. And I guess in some ways it was a functional house church. We had a leadership team and we invited outside leaders to come in and equip our leaders for the task. We ate meals together, worshipped together, took turns guiding the discussions, and took communion every week. But the majority of the people who came (including Kelsey and I) attended a standard church on Sunday mornings, so it felt disingenuous to call it a church plant. However, it was relayed to my pastor that we had planted a church without his guidance or blessing, so a meeting was in order.

One evening Kelsey and I met with our pastor and some other members of the community. By this time, I had been off staff for a year and had settled in as disgruntled, disconnected member. It was the toughest meeting I ever sat through. My pastor was concerned for us, concerned about the home group, concerned with the questions I was asking. He had good reason to be. I was headed down a path he and I both knew was incongruent with the convictions of our church. I was not full-on endorsing the things I once called heresy, but I was no longer able to dismiss the ideas as nonsense. I also could not say firmly, beyond a shadow of a doubt, what I believed anymore. As the conversation went on, I realized I could not fall in line with the rest of the church. The path I was on was the only way I knew anymore, and I realized I was going to have to walk away from my church if I wanted to salvage my faith, not because of any one thing that had been said or done to me—my experience with that community contained much more good than bad—but because I just did not fit anymore.

This church I had been attending since I was eight years old—the place I was baptized, started ministry, preached my first sermon, held my mom's funeral, proposed to and married Kelsey, the community that helped pay bills when finances were tight, bought me a brand-new laptop when my old one crashed, and helped clean up my mom's apartment after she died, the people who raised me and loved me during the darkest and most painful moments of my life—I did not belong with them anymore. And the tragic irony of the whole thing was this: the place where I once received the most revelation from God was now the place God seemed hardest to find. It was nobody's fault, though in my arrogance and anger at the time I thought it was. It was just the new season. My doubts, questions, and hurts were not wrong, but I did not know how to explore them without shame. It hurt, it was messy, and mistakes were made, but it needed to happen. I was being called away, an idea I would have never entertained six months prior to this meeting. In that moment, I knew the only way forward was to leave.

As the meeting drew to a close I could not keep myself from openly weeping. Tears streamed down my face and my voice quaked. I hugged my pastor tight, he called me son, and then we left. I did not account for how difficult it would be to leave my church, but it felt almost as devastating as losing my mom. I didn't make any public statement on social media about leaving. I quietly backed out. And soon my exciting freefall into mystery turned into a full-fledged existential crisis.

Important to Know

Even though I have not returned to this church as a member, there has been wonderful healing in some key relationships there. Particularly between myself and my pastor. We have rekindled our relationship, and he is to this day a friend. While there was a painful season of me walking away, there has been a recrossing of paths and beautiful restoration.

Losing the Bible

It was just a couple weeks after that meeting I was sitting in the hospital room with Jack after he attempted suicide, questioning the justice of hell and the existence of God. I got home from my shift that night, three hours later than I was supposed to. I threw away my blood-stained shirt and sat on the couch next to my wife who had fallen asleep waiting up for me. I started weeping. I was sad, lonely, afraid, and had no God to pray to. It felt like my lifeline had been removed, like my soul was dying. Grieving the choice to walk away from my church, which felt like the only thing I could do at the time, made God feel more inaccessible than ever.

I continued to seek God in the Scriptures. There was a point before all this where my Bible was my meeting place with the Divine. Everytime I opened it I just knew I was in the presence of something holy. But that wasn't the case anymore. I couldn't read more than a page at a time without being confronted with disarming questions and concerns that never bothered me before. The next several weeks led to some disheartening discoveries that did not necessarily boost my confidence in the faith.

Genesis 1 says trees, animals, and birds were created before man, but Genesis 2 says man was created first. Well . . . which was it? Both can't be true at the same time. This lead me to do a Google search of "contradictions in the Bible." I had spent so much of my Christian walk not noticing, ignoring, or explaining away apparent contradictions in Scripture. I was not prepared to find several hundred contradictions I could not explain away after my Google search. I was shocked. I read other Christians' thoughts on the Scriptures, but the majority of their arguments contained a "nothing to see here, move right along" auspice. How could the inerrant, infallible, plenary word of God, which was the final authority on all matters of faith, have *so many* contradictions?

Then I started thinking about the scientific claims of the Bible. We know the earth doesn't rest on pillars as 1 Samuel 2:8 tells us. We've been to space, we have pictures. There's no refuting this without becoming some anti-NASA-truther. The scientific community universally verifies the earth is over 4 billion years old, yet if we take the Bible literally we must conclude the earth is hardly over 8,000 years old. "Well, God made it to look old," I used to say. "You can stain a table to make it look older than it is. God did the same thing to the earth, for aesthetics." That was once a satisfactory retort to the age-of-the-earth question, but now it just made God seem dishonest. Why would you make something look old, knowing it would fool the majority of humanity into thinking wrongly about how long it took you to create the thing? How is that not lying?

Then there's the violence in the Bible. *So much violence.* Genesis 6–8 sees God flooding the entire earth. Because God felt guilty for creating humanity, he killed every man, woman, child, and infant. Millions of bodies floating on the surface of the earth, killed by a God who saw fit to save only one family. Exodus 11–12 sees God using the angel of death to kill all the firstborn in the nation of Egypt, seemingly indiscriminate of age. The entire book of Joshua is the story of what appears to be an attempt at genocide and ethnic cleansing. It's no wonder I and the majority of the Christians around me growing up were totally unphased by the call to support the wars on Iraq and Afghanistan, even though our deity Jesus commanded us to forgive and even bless our enemies. But the commands of Jesus were just a few sentences in a book completely littered with violence.

What to do with all the violence? While Preston's book *Fight* helped a lot with this skirmish, I still had nagging questions about why God would permit or directly cause these atrocities. Looking for answers, I read an article by a reformed theologian whose work I once revered. In his essay titled "Why Did God Command the Children of Israel to Kill Every Man, Woman, and Child in the Promised Land?," R. C. Sproul contends the Canaanites were a threat to the purity of God's people, and

God commanded them all to be put to death because they were all, every man, woman, and child of them, sinners. And the wage of sin is death. In short, God did this for the same reason He does all that He does, for his glory ... When we read about the execution of the Canaanites we ought not ask "How could God do this?" but "Why does God not Kill us all?"

You see, we shouldn't be bothered by the violence in the Old Testament, or even by the horrifying things that happen in our world today, because we deserve worse. I suppose Jack should not be bothered by the rape and torture he was exposed to because, apparently, he deserved a lot worse.

Unsurprisingly, this argument was not very helpful.

I understood the argument which insists that without the removal of people with pagan practices Israel would become corrupted and defiled by their rituals. And that's exactly what happened. Israel failed to remove every person, and just a few books later they too were offering child sacrifices to false gods. But this is *God* we're talking about. Slaughtering countless men, women, and children was the only way to preserve Israel? At the time, the tension was too much for me to bare.

How is any of this at all consistent with the God revealed in Christ, who preached enemy love and turning the other cheek in his famous Sermon on the Mount (Matt 5–7)? Jesus models a God who would rather die for his enemies than kill them. Yet at the direct hands or the command of this God, countless millions of people have died. And that's just in the Bible. This says nothing of the Crusades, the Inquisition, slavery, or the genocide and displacement of Native Americans at the hands of English settlers, all who did what they did with a Bible in their hands and a cross around their necks.

I'm not sure why the violence in the Bible never really bothered me before this. Maybe it did and I don't remember it. Maybe I was sold out on a similar argument R.C. Sproul made. Maybe I just care now because I lost my mom, and I understand the devastating impact of losing a loved one. Maybe seeing accounts of God or people on God's behalf inflict that pain on the masses is just too much for me.

> I wept because the God I had spent so much time worshipping wanted his commands to kill to be carried out so thoroughly that when he was failed, he abandoned his first chosen king.

One night while trying to read my Bible I was reading in 1 Samuel 15. In this chapter, we see Israel's antecedent King Saul rejected by God because he did not succeed in totally destroying the Amalekites. Saul was told to kill every man, woman, child, infant, and animal, and he failed to do so. In failing to do this Saul was all but disowned by God. At this I began weeping. I wept because I too felt disowned by God in that moment. And I wept because the God I had spent so much time worshipping wanted his commands to kill to be carried out so thoroughly that when he was failed, he abandoned his first chosen king. I wept and for the first time put my Bible on my bookshelf.

Silence

The next day was the start of my weekend. My neighbor invited me to attend a debate a local church was hosting between an atheist and a Christian apologist. At first nothing seemed less interesting to me. But I decided to attend as a last-ditch effort to restore my faith. Maybe the atheist would ask the questions I was asking, and maybe the apologist's answers would be what I needed to hear to spark revival in my soul. Maybe I could go back to my church, recant my heresy, and get back to a normal life. I needed to find a way to make all of this real.

The debate was held at a trendy coffee shop in my town. The room was crowded but I found a seat. The debate started and I was immediately put off by the snarky arrogance of both opponents. I sat next to a lady who cheered at everything the atheist said, and sneered whenever the Christian said anything at all (including gushing about how great his wife was). Not wanting to associate with this lady was almost enough to rescue my faith on its own. As the debate went on I grew more disheartened.

Just about everything the atheist was saying made so much more sense to me than what the Christian was saying. I was in shock and struggled to hold back my tears. It was painfully clear to me the atheist was winning the debate. It was clear to him too, because at one point he said to the "apologist" (later I found out he had no formal training, he just read a lot of Lee Strobel) "You know, if you did not try to defend the Bible as a literal science and history book you'd have a much stronger case to make about the beauty of the gospel. You're missing the forest for the trees." To which the apologist responded, "If I can't trust the entirety of Scripture as infallible, I can't trust any of it. If I pick and choose what to believe is true, I take the authority out of the Bible's hands and put it into mine."

And at that point I agreed with him. There was only one problem: I no longer believed the Bible to be a reliable account of history or science. And if I could not trust some of it I could not trust any of it. I drove home from the debate with my heart sunken into my stomach. I parked in my driveway, and closed my eyes to pray. I said, "If you're there I need you to show yourself to me. I can't do this anymore. I'm stuck and I need to move forward. I need a reason to hang on to you, and I need it now."

Nothing.

Silence.

Rage bellowed within me. "Then I'm not wasting my time anymore," I shouted. I got out of my car, and slammed the door, agnostic to any notion of God.

CHAPTER NINE

There I Find You in the Mystery

"Faith isn't about having everything figured out ahead of time; faith is about following the quiet voice of God without having everything figured out ahead of time."
—RACHEL HELD EVANS

"When they saw him, they worshipped him; but some doubted."
—MATTHEW 28:17 (NIV)

Here is All There is

I WOULD SAY I got in a solid month of unbelief before God found a way to get my attention. I did not tell anyone I had stopped believing. I simply moved through life and kept my thoughts and feelings to myself. Even in this time I was haunted by the face of Christ. I did not believe he was someone I could interact with in the present, but as a metaphor I could think of no better idea to latch onto. So, I still tried to follow Jesus in the ways I could. To me this simply meant I latched onto progressivism and humanistic ideas as much as possible. Those philosophies seemed to better bring the ideals of Jesus to the present more than my conservative upbringing. I appreciated podcasts by Rob Bell and The Liturgists during this time because they gave me an avenue to engage with this Jesus I loved so much without having to deny my personal experience of his painful absence.

PART I: BEAUTIFUL FAITH SHACKLED IN SHAME

I thought of Jesus as a sort of human Big Bang. The Big Bang was such a tremendous event it caused the ever-expanding pattern of the universe. Even though this was nearly 14 billion years ago we still see how its echo is continuously shaping our universe. Jesus was the human Big Bang to me. He was such a tremendous force for good that I could still see and feel the echo of his goodness. I could not contribute what I thought of Jesus to the current activity of his Divine Spirit, but the past activity of an extraordinary human.

I was not interested in the smug attitudes of Richard Dawkins or Christopher Hitchens. I did not fall into a category of people who thought all religion was evil and all who follow it are mindless morons. There were no blogs or Facebook posts declaring my newfound unbelief. More than anything I wanted to believe. I did not have any answers. I couldn't tell you why there were moments in my life where, while in the most pain I could imagine, I felt as though God were right there with me. I couldn't tell you why it all stopped making sense to believe in Jesus as a living presence. I hated my doubt, but I couldn't find a way to faith.

For a while I functioned as an agnostic; not in crisis over my faith, no weeping and yelling at God, just a quiet mourning in my heart over the loss of my Healer. An emptiness I thought would never be mended. I lost my God, but I was finding some semblance of calm after a few turbulent years. I did not desire to go live out every debauched impulse I felt. Before, I thought I needed my faith to live with any moral compass, but I was relieved to realize as an agnostic I did not want to cheat on my wife, start using heroin, start worshipping Satan, or go clubbing baby seals. To my surprise, on the other side of faith I was still me.

I found myself more appreciative of the things that were in front of me. As a Christian, everything was about waiting to experience the fullness of joy until God took me to heaven. I viewed all satisfaction experienced on earth as faulty compared to what I hoped to experience after I died. I did not seriously appreciate creation, because God would come and destroy it all anyways. Any connection I made with someone who did not share my faith led me to planning the ways I could convert them and be a witness, or it led me to keep my distance from them lest they lead me astray.

This was not the case anymore. I could stop, look at a sunset, and be moved to tears by its beauty. I could walk by a river and listen to the streams like it was an orchestral piece that creation was composing just for me. I literally stopped and smelled the roses. I treasured every new person I met, and desired nothing more than to know them and their messy, beautiful, scary stories. I was more in the moment than I had been in my whole life. There was no time like the present. I only had those moments, and I would never get them back or experience better after I died. So, I was forced to savor them. I related to people without feeling the pressure to change or judge them. Taking time to observe nature and people through a lens of awe and wonder somehow filled the church-shaped hole in my heart.

I was astounded to find my time as an unbeliever profoundly livable. At the time, I thought it was because I did not need God anymore. Later I would learn it was because I was slowly discovering aspects of God I had never seen before. Because, even if in the trenches of my mind I could not muster the strength to believe, God was with me, and I marveled at his beauty and goodness without even knowing it. When we are awe struck by creation: a sunset, a flower, a person . . . it really is as if we are awestruck by God. I thought I was alone, but God was in the sunset, God was in melody of the river, God was in the aromatic scent of the flowers, his glory bursting onto the colorful petals. God was in the men and women I met, with his image shimmering through their smiles, sorrows, beauty, and pain. I experienced God even as an unbeliever.

However, my would-be agnosticism was short-lived.

Mosaic in the Making

Jack made a quick recovery after his suicide attempt. He was out of the hospital in no time, and pursued his counseling, schooling, and health with fresh fervor. Despite his best attempts he was alive and had a new lease on life. He seemed to move his way through life with joy. He was less confrontational, angry, and depressed. He was motivated and vibrant. One evening we took him and some of the other boys in the house to one of the buttes in Eugene, just to get some time away from the building.

It was night time and the lights in the city of Eugene shimmered gold and silver. Jack and I walked behind the rest of the group. I said to him "You are doing so well. I'm so proud of you."

"Thank you!" he responded, "I feel well."

"What happened?" I asked. "Where did all of this positivity come from?"

He stopped and leaned against a fence that separated the summit of the butte from a downhill slope. He looked at the lights of the city with a sort of half smile on his face. Then he responded, "Do you know what mosaics are?"

"Sure" I responded.

"Well," he paused as he searched for the right words, "it's like, when I didn't die I realized I was a mosaic. I have all of this brokenness. And before all I could see was how broken I was. But now... I don't know how to explain it, but I just sense there is something out there helping me turn my broken pieces into something beautiful, like a mosaic. I'm not hearing voices or anything, but something from outside myself is telling me my story can have a really beautiful turn in it. I am confident I am going to have everything I need in order to be who I want to be, and that I'm cared for. For the first time in so long, I feel safe. I never thought I could believe in God, but doesn't that sound like it could be him?"

"Yeah, it does," I said sheepishly, trying to hold back tears. I had not told him, or anyone, that I did not believe in God anymore. But even if I didn't believe anymore, the kid had given me something to consider. What was this thing that was communicating so much value to him? I wanted to just dismiss it as him getting a new lease on life after a near-death experience. But there was something else going on; deep within my heart I felt a sensation I had not felt in a long time. It was similar to the sensation I felt the night God told me "nothing stands between us." The feeling was not as strong or disruptive as it was that night all those years ago, but it was just as present. It was the familiar voice of a long-lost friend, and in my heart I began to notice the sparks of resurrection.

I drove home from work that night, more tears streaming and more thoughts racing. I sat in my car after pulling into our parking lot. I was so sure I was done with this, but the feeling of an old friend coming home grew exponentially in my car. I didn't have words to say, only the experience of God showing me I had not been abandoned, and neither had Jack.

I had gone a month without talking to God, to this day the longest we have ever gone without speaking. I leaned my head back against the headrest of my car, and began to pray:

"I don't know what to think about you anymore. I don't know who or what you are. But you won't leave me alone. Are you the spark, the hope, the presence I feel in this moment? You revealed yourself as love to me when I was four years old. You pushed through all my shame and self-hatred when I was sixteen to tell me you saw and loved all of me. And now, you're telling this kid who has every reason to want to die that he can make something beautiful out of his life, and you're willing to help. Why do you come and go so much? Did you ever really come? Did you ever really go? I can't know for sure who you are, but I think, I hope you're Jesus. And I don't know how to go about knowing you, but if you're the thing pushing healing into mine and this kid's world, I will spend the rest of my life dedicated to finding you, sharing you, and following you. It's nice to see you again."

And with that, I dried my eyes and got out of my car. I walked to the door of my apartment, with a little more faith in my heart, and a little more hope in my life.

Won't Let You Go

The days following my interaction with God in my car were not filled with the Spirit-filled jubilance I would have hoped for. My heart still ached with doubt. I couldn't pick up my Bible without being crushed with more questions than answers, and the idea of stepping into a church made my body quake with anxiety. I tried to pray, but I didn't even know how to talk to God anymore. I didn't know who or what I was talking to, or if I was talking to anyone or anything at all. Trying to strap any definitions to the Divine only seemed to rob my experience of it. Putting God into categories also felt constricting. I would not find God where I once did, not yet. At the time, this was a tireless and exasperating experience, but looking back I see God was showing me new ways of interacting with him. Relying on my old religious habits wouldn't do the trick this time around. If I was going to rebuild my faith house I needed a new set of tools before I could rediscover value in the old ones.

Not knowing where to find God, or if there was any God to find, made me feel abandoned. When I was sixteen and thought I had lost it all, God tracked me down, and seemed to elevate my consciousness to a new reality. I sensed the Spirit and her activity everywhere. However, this time, I still felt hollow. I wanted to walk with God like Adam did in the garden. I wanted to be so satisfied in the Spirit that I would not need or want anything else, but that's not what I got. Even though I had a moment that made faith seem possible for me I felt a deep sense of abandonment.

Still, I prayed, though my prayers looked vastly different. Whereas my prayers were once petitions for God to show me healings, prophecies, miracles, not to send me to hell, and for freedom from my sexuality, now my prayers were the groans of a soul caught in a dark night.

PART I: BEAUTIFUL FAITH SHACKLED IN SHAME

"Why don't you seem constant? Why do you come and go like the ocean tide? I need you. Where can I find you?"

Around this time, July of 2016, my favorite band—Switchfoot—released a new album. As per my tradition every time they released an album, I sat on my couch with the lyric book in my hand and headphones in my ears. It was a warm summer evening in our little apartment. As I sat on our living room couch Kelsey laid her head on my lap and she watched her show while our dog Halpert (named after Jim) lay at our feet. I started the album. I was not let down. Each track was a meaningful reminder as to why this group has continued to be my favorite band since middle school. I finished up their Rumi-inspired song "Where the Light Shines Through" with a smile on my face. By this point Kelsey was fast asleep. Then the next track began: calm and light electric guitar picking, a smooth atmospheric synth in the background, and then the intro of Jon Foreman singing in his gentlest cadence. He began to sing the words my soul needed to hear.

Through the song "I Won't Let You Go" I was invited to go further up and further in with God. I was invited to acknowledge my doubts and questions, my hurts and betrayals, and I was urged to move through them. Maybe the things that happened to me were not reliable indicators of who God was. Maybe I had not been abandoned. When I could not pray to God the song felt as though it was God's prayer for me. Before, music was not the place I turned to hear what God would say to me. "It stirs the emotions, but it is not the Word of God," I would say (I could be such an unpleasant person). If it did not come from the Bible or contain direct references to the Bible, I would not receive it on the same level as God speaking to me through the Scriptures. But here I was. Weeping quietly to myself as I felt the Spirit singing Jon Foreman's words to my heart.

Maybe the shame I experienced because of my sexuality, maybe being forced to watch my mom slowly succumb to the horrors of America's opioid epidemic, maybe the emptiness of not having a community, maybe the constant bouncing between the depression and rage I felt about how my life had turned out, maybe these things were not signs God had stood idly by as the world around me crumbled. Maybe the fact I still held breath in my lungs and hope in my heart and longed for a deeper faith were all signs to the contrary. Maybe my soul longs for God because my soul was designed to be connected to God. Maybe God hadn't let me go. Maybe in God I lived, moved, and had my being. Maybe it was time to doubt my doubts, and open myself up to the possibility that I had been seeing things the wrong way.

It's possible all of creation is just an accident. It's possible we are just a conglomeration of earth and water, dust and air. It's possible I only believe in God because I want to believe. Maybe I've tricked my brain into telling my emotions to respond to certain triggers that make it feel as though I'm having an encounter with the Divine. It's possible all the pain in my life and the much deeper pain many experience throughout the world testify only to a chaotic and disorderly universe without an Intelligent Designer. That is all entirely possible. But it's also possible I really have met God. It's possible there really is this Spirit at work in the world that came in the human body of Jesus, and this Spirit is still speaking today. It's possible God really is the Ultimate Reality, and the deepest truths are discovered when the Divine is acknowledged as our Ground of Being. Maybe Jack, that kid in the halfway house who was more a victim than a criminal, really was experiencing the redemptive movements of the Spirit. Maybe God really was healing my soul and forgiving my sins. Maybe there is meaning to all of this. Maybe Something is pushing the human project forward.

How do I know what is true? At the time, I couldn't know for sure. But I did know one thing: I could choose what to believe. There isn't a person alive who hasn't bought into some bigger story to make sense of their reality. And I could not think of a better one than the story of Jesus to help me make sense of mine.

That night as I listened to a song that felt as though my favorite band had written it specifically for me, I was reminded of something that became the starting point of my reconstruction: God had not let me go. He was hanging on to me, and it was time I started hanging on to him.

Life Rafts of Faith and Hope

The task of putting back together my Christianity proved to be an intimidating one, but I had great guides to help me. I continued to read books and digest podcasts like they were my life source, and in a lot of ways they were. Kelsey and I began attending a church again, and I started spending a lot of time with the pastor there. He had gone through his own deconstructive experience and he put the pieces back together so beautifully that I wanted what he had. Tim taught me how to hang on to Christ as I continued to fall into the mystery. Things got put back together, and then torn apart, and then put back together again. Some things were tossed aside never to be revisited (I don't see myself returning to Calvinism anytime soon). Other things came quickly, and came back stronger than before.

My pastor introduced me to the writings of a Franciscan friar named Richard Rohr. His book *The Naked Now* was particularly important to me at the beginning of my reconstruction. The book taught me the lesson of finding God in the mystery, and it gave me new avenues to discover the Divine. I was given the freedom to look at all of my "I don't knows" as the endless places God could show up, rather than as the places I could not see him. They are right when they say giving into skepticism is a slippery slope. It is a muscle that, once flexed, feels nearly impossible to shut down. I struggled deeply with not feeling certain about any of the faith claims I tried to make. I couldn't be certain Christ rose from the dead. I couldn't be certain God had any part in the compilation of the Bible. I couldn't be certain the doctrines and creeds the church has passed down for so many years held any credibility or authority.

I didn't know.

And that was okay, because God was not asking for my certainty. God has never asked for our certainty, God wants our faith. Ephesians 2:8 doesn't say, "For it is by grace through *certainty* you have been saved." Nonsense! Rather, it says, "It is by grace through *faith* you have been saved." As Anne Lamott wrote in her book *Plan B*, "The opposite of faith is not doubt, it is certainty." I think that idea bleeds with truth, for what need do the certain have for faith?

Allowing faith and doubt to coexist changes one's perception of mystery. Rather than a deep, dark abyss that seeks to swallow faith, mystery becomes the ocean of God's goodness, and we are invited to swim in it. God is infinitely mysterious. This does not make him endlessly unknowable, but endlessly knowable. Faith and hope have become my life rafts as I struggle through the waves of doubt (and let me tell you, I still struggle through those waves), because even if I can't know for sure if all of this is true, I can hope it is. Even if I can't always claim total certainty in my spiritual walk, I can have faith in it. And the more I disentangle the radical, inclusive, world-healing love of Jesus from American evangelicalism the easier this all gets. In fact, this tension-filled marriage of doubt and faith is oftentimes the place I get to see God the clearest.

The weight I place on the role of embracing tension and mystery in the Christian life is why I believe the 2011 movie *The Tree of Life* (starring

Brad Pitt, Sean Penn, and Jessica Chastain) is one of the greatest sermons ever preached. I have come across no other work of art that so brilliantly captures the love, fear, grace, beauty, chaos, tension, and majesty of trying to perceive how God is working from the limited perspectives of our own humanity. It's my favorite movie of all time, and every viewing feels like a holy moment.

This new way of seeing and perceiving God brought so much increase into my life. An increase of the Presence, and increase of being present. It forced me to examine myself more and see how God was speaking through my emotions, but more than anything it forced me in to a place of theological humility. Before, I was so sure I was right and so convinced anyone who disagreed with me was not only mistaken, but dangerously misled. This is not to say I have embraced an amorphous ideology which claims all truth is relative, but it does mean I can readily confess when it comes to many topics of faith, "I don't know."

Perhaps this is why the great sages, mystics, and prophets throughout history have spoken of God through metaphor. When it comes to defining something as broad as Ultimate Reality there are times when it is most appropriate to say, "God is like . . ." God is not a literal Shepherd, King, Father, Rock, or Hen . . . these are all biblical metaphors used to describe God because literal language is too limiting. When one stands before the Mystery all one has to cling to is metaphor.

Speaking through Silence

It was January of 2017, and Martin Scorsese's movie *Silence* (spoilers ahead if you haven't seen it) had just hit wide release. I had been tracking the production of this movie for years. Scorsese is one of my favorite filmmakers (I know this is not a hot take for fellow film buffs), and him taking on the subject of a Christian missionary wrestling through a crisis of faith felt like a Godsend during the season of life I was in. Eager to watch the movie as soon as we could, Dennis, Jordan, and I opted to make the two-hour drive to Portland, the closest city it was playing in. If I ever need to spot God's grace in my life I can recall that I have two best friends who will make a two-hour drive to watch an independent, contemplative, existential movie with me.

So, we risked the icy roads and overpaid for our tickets. The movie started and it instantly captured me with its raw, stylistic vision. *Silence* follows two Jesuit priests (played by Andrew Garfield and Adam Driver) from Spain to Japan, where Christians are ruthlessly persecuted. They enter this dangerous terrain with the mission of finding their mentor (Liam Neeson), who supposedly had renounced the faith. What follows is two hours and forty minutes of some of the most honest dialogue on belief and disbelief I have ever seen. The movie reads as Martin Scorsese's confession of faith (and doubt).

Throughout the movie you see several people readily giving their lives to death in order to avoid renouncing their faith. I ached in my heart as I was forced to confront how much more seriously these characters took their faith than I did. I was a Christian whose faith was expressed by my self-righteous Facebook and Twitter posts. I raged and complained about the ways other Christians poorly represented Jesus, but never put myself in uncomfortable territory for the sake of the gospel. All of a sudden my angst-filled internet rants felt like an insulting imitation of the real thing as I watched these characters honestly wrestle with what they believed, and what it was costing them.

By the end of the movie we have seen the main character, Father Rodrigues, in physical and spiritual torture as he grapples with the apparent silence of God in the face of so many dying in his name. Rodrigues makes a lot of difficult choices, some of which bring more pain to the people around him, but by the end we see that through it all Christ has held on to him. And by the final frame, we see that in the end he too was holding on to Christ. Rodrigues makes choices that could lead anyone to believe Christ would want nothing to do with him, nor he with Christ. But in the final frame of the film we see how he hung on, symbolized by the character clutching a tiny crucifix in his hands at the end of his life.

Now, I don't mind admitting I have no problem crying for the right movie, but at the end of this movie I was practically inconsolable. Not just because the movie is fantastic (the movie is *fantastic*), but because I felt the last big hurdle in my faith had been addressed. I knew God was hanging on to me during my crisis of faith, I believed Jesus had promised me he would never let me go, but I had let him go, and not because I had a crisis of faith and deconstructed—I let him go long before that.

My deconstruction was the next inevitable step after my years as an arrogant bully of a Christian. Ten years before I watched this movie I was a terrified, depressed, shame-filled sixteen-year-old kid on the verge of suicide, and God broke through my darkness to make one thing loud and clear: demonstrated by the cross, nothing stood between us but love. Eleven years before that I became aware of this God because I grew conscious of a love greater than even that of my mother. The fire that raged in my heart after those experiences was one of passionate love for my Creator, and it birthed in me a desire to show my Creator's love to the people around me. This was the hum in my soul that got me through every major pain and doubt in my life. The reason behind the vast mysteries and complexities of creation and existence were made understandable to an innocent child, and then to a terrified teenager who had lost that innocence.

> All the metaphor and language we try to come up with to describe the indescribable is futile, but when we look at Jesus we see it plain as day: God is love.

All the metaphor and language we try to come up with to describe the indescribable is futile, but when we look at Jesus we see it plain as day: God is love. God creates and hangs on to his creation, because he loves his creation. God came in a feeble human body, taking on all our sorrows and weaknesses, and demonstrated everything we need to know about God with his life, teachings, death, and resurrection. God sent his Spirit so we too can incarnate that love dressed in skin and bone.

I let that go. I traded it for the thrill that comes with feeling theologically superior to the people around me. I traded experience with God for certainty about God. I traded security for fear and shame. I traded love for doctrine. I stopped looking at Jesus as the clearest revelation of who God is, and allowed myself to fall into the trap of degrading God to nothing more than an exercise in intellectual assent. And even after I tore apart all the things I thought were keeping me away from God, I realized even in my deconstruction and reconstruction, I was still not hanging on to Christ. I was hanging on to my ability to make sense of it all, unwilling to submit myself to the Mystery. Watching this movie forced me to confront the reality of the preciousness of my faith. I needed to stop approaching my faith as a disengaged riddle, and start seeing it as an invitation to observe what Jesus did, and to go and do likewise. It wasn't enough to believe the right things about God anymore. I left the theater with a thought I could not shake: *Following Jesus matters.*

Part II

A Faith Worth Passing Down

CHAPTER TEN

The Donkey, the Elephant, and the Lamb

"Jesus' resurrection is the beginning of God's new project, not to snatch people away from earth to heaven, but to colonize earth with the life of heaven. That, after all, is what the Lord's Prayer is about."

—N. T. WRIGHT

"The time has come. The kingdom of God has come near. Repent, and believe the good news!"

—MARK 1:15 (NIV)

Uncanny Valley Christianity

THE SUN BEAMS ITS brilliant rays onto the golden sands of the Judean Desert. Around this time in the afternoon the sweaty carpenter would normally be found under the cool shade of a fig tree enjoying his lunch, but not today. He is halfway through a forty-day fast in the middle of the desert. As he walks and prays, the Son of Man wonders why the Spirit would lead him to such a desolate place.

Many of us have been there, haven't we? We were confident we had responded to God's call for our lives, only to feel as though we were called to nothing more than torment.

Hungry, weak, and tired, the son of Mary recalls the cool waters of his baptism just a few weeks earlier. He remembers the heavens opening up, and the Holy Spirit appearing like a dove. His eyes well with tears as he recalls the voice of love telling him on that day, "You are my dearly beloved son, you bring me great joy" (Matt 3:17 NIV).

He presses on, uncertain but full of faith.

Step after step the warm sand burns through his sandals. His stomach growls and he sighs in sorrow. He then senses the familiar presence of evil, a presence that has loomed over his shoulder his whole life. The carpenter discerns this presence has one goal: to prevent him from accomplishing the mission of uniting heaven and earth. This devil launches his first assault, "If you are the son of God . . ." (Matt 4:3 NIV).

There's the first attack. Did you catch it? The deadly "if" which calls into question how beloved we really are.

You know how the rest of the story goes as recorded in both Matthew and Luke 4. First the devil tempts Jesus with bread, which is low-hanging fruit on the devil's part since Jesus hadn't eaten in weeks. After that doesn't work, Satan offers Jesus authority over all the kingdoms of the world. Now, remember Jesus' context: he was an occupant who spent his whole life suffering, and watching his people suffer, under the oppression of the Roman empire. I'm sure Jesus would have loved to use this as an opportunity to bring justice to his people. Even still Jesus resists the power of the evil one. Finally, Satan brings Jesus to the top of the highest point of the temple. He taunts Jesus, "If you really are the son of God, then jump. God will surely send angels to protect you" (Matt 4:6 NIV).

Jesus, again, resists.

Bread, worldly power, the protection of God himself . . . while these three things are certainly particular to Jesus and his context, Satan is offering something every human being wants. Jordan puts it this way: Satan is tempting Jesus with three P's: Prosperity, power, and protection. We all want prosperity, power, and protection, and many will make great sacrifices and compromises to receive those things for them and theirs. If Jesus had taken the devil up on any of those offers, the whole mission would have been compromised and we could be living in a scarily different world. Jesus was able to say no to receiving those things from the devil because he knew God would provide them.

In our country, many of us who claim to be followers of Jesus have failed where Christ triumphed. Have we taken the devil up on his bribes for prosperity, power, and protection? These things on their own are not inherently evil, but anything snatched from the devil's hand will be manipulated for evil. We need to examine the consequences our quest for the three P's has had on the American church, and the role that plays in the mass exodus Christian communities have experienced. I have said a few times by now, and will say a few times more, most people don't deconstruct because of Jesus. Many who experience the turbulence of deconstruction resonate with the sentiments attributed to Gandhi when he said, "I like your Christ. I do not like your Christians. Your Christians are so unlike your Christ."

In the 1970s, Masahiro Mori, a professor at the Tokyo Institute of Technology, coined a term known as the *uncanny valley*. He used the term to describe the phenomena people experience when they see robots that are so lifelike it invokes feelings of fear, unease, and suspicion. More recently we experienced the uncanny valley in movies like *Rogue One: A Star Wars Story*, in which the digitally recreated Grand Moff Tarkin and a digitally de-aged Princess Leia appeared on the screen. Looking at them, we know intuitively that the original actor to play Tarkin, Peter Cushing, passed away a long time ago, and we know that by the time the film was released Carrie Fisher had aged well beyond how Leia looks in this film. Yet in spite of knowing this, their facial features were recreated so well it is hard to specifically point out the things about their appearance that give away the fact that these are not the beloved actors, but digital recreations. I fear many of us have embraced an uncanny valley expression of Christianity. I know I did.

In the next two chapters I am going to address some hot-button issues, like politics and racism. Why am I doing this? Because the Christian worldview I so aggressively clung to did not have an adequate posture toward these things when I held them up to scrutiny. My faith identity was rooted more in a conservative American identity than it was a Christ-centered one. These two things, politics and faith, were so entangled that once I grew disenchanted with the corruption I saw in my world leaders, I also grew disenchanted with Jesus. As I started listening to the stories of people of color, and seeing the ways in which racism is alive and well today, I did not have an adequate response. My faith was centered on waiting until I died so I could go to some other place in some other time. My priorities were not to bring justice into the world, but to get as many people as I could to come with me to heaven.

I bring politics and racism into this conversation because Jesus actually has a lot to teach about these things, and what he has to offer is such good news, so much better than ignoring societal injustices and following a tainted political ideology like it could save the soul of the world. The worldview I embraced was a sort of uncanny valley version of Christianity: it had the appearance of Christianity, but when the rubber met the road it did not feel very Christian. My hope in the second part of this book is to unpack a vision for a faith worth passing down. It is all too easy to abandon a faith that fails to provide helpful direction and response to the injustices folks experience every day on a societal level, but that is not the historic Christian faith. Following Jesus should actually have some very real-world implications. Most people don't deconstruct because of Jesus. Most people deconstruct because the cognitive dissonance they experience is too much to handle. It should not be this way, and it doesn't have to be.

I want to make clear that while I will be analyzing the impact of American Christianity on my life during the 2016 election and the victory of Donald Trump, I want to encourage you not to take this as a sign that I hold faith in the Democratic Party as the best great hope of the world. As I will explain shortly, I am a follower of Jesus exiled to Babylon, and both sides of the political spectrum are led by Babylonian leaders clamoring for power. My hope is to go beyond chumming the surface of political rhetoric, and point Christ-following people toward a more Christlike way. I will not be scrutinizing Hillary Clinton or the Democratic Party as heavily because, quite frankly, it would be strange for me to do that. I am not qualified for such a task. That is not my world. I don't experience existential whiplash over the failings of Democrat leaders because I was conditioned from birth to expect very little from them. The alternative I propose to allegiance to republicanism is not an allegiance to liberalism, but to Jesus. They say you should write what you know, and I know very well what it's like to be a Christian sold-out on conservative ideology, only to have that ideology lead me to a dead end.

The End of Christendom

For many, there is enough baggage in the marriage of Christianity and politics to make it easier to disregard both altogether. Or, as often happens, many see the casualties of Christian power in culture and reject Christianity for a humanistic philosophy. Humanists are those who place a primary value on humanity over the Divine, and seek only rational ways to aid humanity. During my time of doubt and deconstruction I observed the ways in which Christians pursuing power had afflicted those on the margins of society. I saw how LGBTQ+ folks were at greater risk of suicide in religious communities than they were in secular culture. I saw how Christians in positions of power advocated for policies and systems that consistently prevented minority groups from attaining positions of privilege (and don't think I'm only poo-pooing Republican leaders here, can someone say Clinton's 1994 crime bill?). I saw how media conglomerates encouraged good people to abandon Jesus' way of peace, love, and justice for the ways of war, fear, and oppression. I noticed almost a sense of apathy in me and my circles whenever the next tragedy took place, content to send out thoughts and prayers but not concerned enough to take action. How could those who worship the God of light also be culpable with such darkness?

Being ill-informed as I was, it was simple for me to dismiss Christianity as the problem. The religion I touted seemed so preoccupied with theories and theologies of the next life, it had little effect on this one. After some investigation, I came to realize this was not a result of authentic and historic Christianity. This was a result of *Christendom*. Christendom, as Stuart Murray Williams say in his book *The Naked Anabaptist*, is when Christianity bends to have coherence with its culture rather than being counterculture. It is what happens when Christians exchange the way of Jesus for the ways of empire, which is obsession with power, affluence, and influence in society. While Christlike service may result in places of influence for some, that is never the goal of following Jesus. Following Jesus is not a means to an end; following Jesus is the end. Christendom refuses to see Christ as a king whose teachings are the way of life, and it reduces him to a get-out-of-hell-free card. Christendom has been seduced into ways of greed, violence, and oppression that early Christians would have rejected as apostasy. In his work, *A Contribution to the Critique of Hegel's Philosophy of Right*, Karl Marx referred to religion as *the opium of the masses*. To Marx, religion (and the promise of paradise after death) was the means by which powerful rulers would prevent their subjects from attempting to stop their violence and oppression. Under Christendom the Marxist critique finds some validation. As N. T. Wright wrote in his most influential work, *Surprised by Hope*,

> A piety (or religion) that sees death as the moment of 'going home at last,' the time when we are 'called into God's eternal peace,' has no quarrel with power mongers who want to carve up the world to suit their own ends.

PART II: A FAITH WORTH PASSING DOWN

This is not to say we reject theology of the afterlife, clearly Jesus had an established construction of the afterlife. But we must stop viewing the Christian call as a call to biding one's time until heaven comes in some other place, in some other time. The Bible starts in the garden of Eden, which is a depiction of the perfect unity between heaven and earth. The Bible ends with a reunification of God's space and human space. We are to infiltrate earth with the life of heaven. This means what we do on earth and how we steward creation matters, and will be called into account when Christ returns.

As Christians continue to lose culture war after culture war it is clear Christendom is on the decline. The temptation for many who are used to holding the most dominant positions in a society is to panic and cry persecution; that is certainly what the *God's Not Dead* movies would have us believe is taking place. However, before we make social martyrs of ourselves, maybe the decline of Christendom is a saving grace. The church has always thrived when it existed on the margins. If Jesus came as what the world would regard as a great and powerful figure, like a Pharaoh, Caesar, or President, it would make sense for Christians to seek the social, political, and military power Christendom has held in our country. But Jesus did not come boasting worldly greatness; he came boasting a power the world regarded (and still does) as foolishness. The Jesus way to power is by taking up your cross for the sake of the world, not seeking to dominate the world. The world's path to power more often than not leads to death. "The cross is foolishness to those who are perishing," as the apostle Paul wrote in his first letter to the Corinthians (1:18 NIV). The quest for power and dominance is a quest that leads one away from the path of Christ.

Any influence or affluence we are granted is intended to be used in service of moving the human project forward. What was true for Abraham is still true for us: we are blessed to be a blessing. Jesus was neither a military strategist nor a valiant warrior, he did not come on an impressive steed wielding a sword and seeking blood; he came wearing dirty sandals washing dirty feet for dirty people. Later, in the Revelation of John, Jesus would come on a steed with a sword, and he was covered in blood. However, the blood would not be the blood of his enemies, but his own blood, symbolizing how Christ gains power by laying down his life for his enemies. And he would not wield the sword with his hands, rather it would come out of his mouth, symbolizing his authority to discern right and wrong, and his ability to speak truth to power.

My faith did not unravel because I had a problem with Jesus. I did not remove myself from Christianity because I felt Jesus was harmful to creation. Much of what accounted for my loss of faith came because I could not imagine a way of following Jesus that did not also include the baggage of violent, greedy, power-hungry leaders who used religion as a means of gaining influence. The fall of Christendom does not mean the end of the church; it is a sign of rebirth. It is an invitation for the church to surrender power by worldly standards and follow Jesus into the generous way of life which brings about human flourishing on every level.

This Ain't My American Dream

*Warning: we're about to talk politics.

*Yes, that means I will be offering a critique of Donald Trump, but do not take this critique as a sign that I think the Democratic Party is an accurate representation of what it means to a Christian in America—that could not be further from the truth. If you are a Trump supporter, and are adamant that President Trump is above critique, or if you are experiencing political fatigue, feel free to move on to the next chapter. However, if you keep reading I think you will see where I'm coming from. The heart of this chapter is less to offer a critique about Donald Trump than it is to offer a critique about myself. Keep reading, bear with me, and you'll see what I mean.

Throughout 2016 I saw something unique take place in myself and many of my evangelical friends. There was this restless sense of frustration with older generations in the church and the way the political landscape was being shaped. Election cycles have been an ugly, cut-throat game for much longer than I've been alive. I remember mercilessly ridiculing friends of mine for having parents who supported Al Gore, and I wasn't even ten years old. Yet there was this shared feeling in our bones that this time around was different. Maybe we were finally old enough to truly see how damaging American political rhetoric can be, or maybe we were actually in a unique cultural moment. There was a growing sense of disenfranchisement as the race to the presidential office went into full swing. Why the disenfranchisement? Because as evangelicals we were taught the importance of family values, kindness, honesty, character, and love, and it seemed the political party in which we were brought up was being co-opted by a man who embodied none of these traits, and our religious communities were

PART II: A FAITH WORTH PASSING DOWN

paving the way for him. Every time a racist, sexist, xenophobic, or ablest remark was made it was excused or defended by the people who taught us those things were wrong. I wasn't alone in feeling like I was being gas-lit by conservative America.

I have no interest in scapegoating, vilifying, or demeaning people who voted for Donald Trump. I do not believe Trump supporters are bad, evil, or without cause. I see and understand the reasons people would want someone like him in office. I know in today's polarizing landscape just saying that is a divisive statement, but I am not interested in catering to American political tribes.

I started off 2016 very much a proud Republican. I trusted Fox News. Ronald Reagan was my favorite president. I revered the likes of Sean Hannity and Bill O'Reilly. Up to this point it absolutely stupefied me that somebody could be a Christian and not be a Republican. Growing up as deeply in conservative American Christianity as I did, the two were so intertwined I did not know it was possible to separate them. It seemed clear to me: Republicans cared about family values and stopping the death of unborn babies; Democrats sought to dismantle the family unit and seemed to advocate for the death of the unborn. Conservatives cared about work ethic and building up a sustainable people who could fend for themselves; liberals wanted to give free handouts to people who were too lazy to get real jobs. My understanding at the time was Democrats wanted to keep lower-class people dependent on the government so they could continually be reelected and maintain their power. For most of my life it was easy for me to buy into the myth that Christian and Republican were practically synonymous.

It was as simple as that for me until the 2016 election when I realized just how erroneous this myth really was. Donald Trump became the candidate for the Republican Party, and then my president—a feat that could not have been accomplished without the unwavering support of evangelical Christians. Donald Trump, for many, is the brash, say-it-like-it-is, nonpolitical hero they have been waiting for. He gave voice to the concerns of middle- to lower-class white America, a demographic who largely went unseen and unheard during the Obama years, and Trump offering them a voice is not a bad thing. Yet the tactics of fear-mongering, racism, and sexism that were used to win the favor of so many in my tribe was disorienting. Rather than appealing to things which reflected Jesus, stuff like neighborly love, generosity, kindness, forgiveness, hope, and inclusion, Trump appealed to the collective fear and anger in evangelical America, which, again, would not be an issue for me if he wasn't lauded by so many as "God's man." He offered provision, power, and protection, and we took it. And whether you consider it a tragedy or a triumph that Donald Trump entered the White House on the votes of evangelicals, if you are an evangelical, you must reckon with what kind of witness this sends the rest of the world.

It was around this time that I started reading Jesus more seriously and deconstructing (it's funny how those two things can happen at the same time). With the exception of his claims to be pro-life, I did not see anything in the Trump campaign that had much to do with Jesus. In spite of this, evangelical heavyweights like Franklin Graham, Jerry Falwell Jr., and James Dobson not only pledged unwavering support, but made him out to be the President that would save the soul of America. Conservative Christians chose him out of the several other seemingly decent conservative Christian candidates, and none of it made any sense to me. When I would point this out the automated response seemed to be, "We elected a president, not a pastor," which is all fine and good if this had been the posture we took for every president we've ever had. But whenever Obama did something immoral in the eyes of my community, we certainly held him to the same standard as that of a pastor.

The Trump phenomenon was inconvenient timing during my deconstruction. My angsty ideological toils seemed to be given a new validation every time Trump said something abhorrent and evangelicals rallied to defend him. I took this as permission to loop all conservatives together, and attempted to separate myself from them as much as possible (there's that sneaky *them* word again). So, I decided to make the jump into progressivism. At the time, it was easier for me to reconcile Jesus' teachings with progressivism than it was with conservative ideology. All the annoyance, intolerance, and suspicion I felt toward progressives a year earlier switched to feeling that way toward conservatives.

As I sought to cling to whatever bits of faith I could, it was easier to do while switching camps. Christ advocated for the poor while the leaders in conservatism championed policies that appeared to keep the poor in their station. I could show concern for refugees, the environment, and equality of all sorts and feel totally justified, because I had verses and Jesus. Conversations switched to the ways in which conservative politics seemed antithetical to the teachings of Christ.

PART II: A FAITH WORTH PASSING DOWN

This is Progress?

The interesting thing about being in a tribe is the way we seem unaware of a factor called *confirmation bias*. Confirmation bias is the tendency to search for, interpret, or favor information in a way that confirms a preexisting belief or assumption, and it is an error in inductive reasoning. With confirmation bias, someone will take in information and, if they agree with the data, they will ignore any flaws in the research so as to maintain their worldview. If they do not agree with the data, they will find reasons the research is flawed, and ignore it all together. It is possible to align yourself with a religion, political party, or movement and not fall into the confirmation bias trap, but it is extremely difficult. My journey into progressivism did not include me shaking my biases when taking in information.

The problem with unchecked confirmation bias is that so much of the time we don't even know we are being suckered into it. We are told the news sources we engage with take an objective approach. CNN touts "facts first" and yet the slant they give their reports appeals primarily to Democrats. Fox News boasts about being "fair and balanced," and yet the only people who seem to buy that rhetoric are Republicans. Objectivity is a guise the press uses to avoid taking responsibility for spreading propaganda while calling it news. "Facts first" and "fair and balanced" are effective ways to tickle ears and tell the consumers they are being fed objective truth, not confirmation bias pornography while we make money for them. News stations are selling a product to advertisers, and that product is you.

After watching the movie *Silence*, I experienced a revival of sorts in my soul, yet I wasn't always aware of how to channel it. I felt as though God was calling me toward a more robust conviction in the story of Jesus, but I was apprehensive to embrace it. I was Mr. Robust before, and I found that I had built my life on a house of cards. Additionally, the writers and podcasters I was looking to the most during this time did not seem to have a conviction in a Christian identity that moved much beyond social justice, and that's where the buck stopped for me as well. Now, to be fair, I question a person's commitment to following Jesus if it doesn't lead to substantial concern for social justice, but my soul was also telling me there was more in Christianity for me to recover.

This would require me adding definitions to many ideas I had let fall by the wayside, or had even grown cynical toward. Because I was unsure of so much, it was hard for me to see God as more than Loving Mystery (which, to this day, I think is a pretty comprehensive definition of the Divine). This was convenient because it allowed me to embrace some form of a pluralistic worldview. I had an aversion to the idea of Christian doctrine having a patent on God. By this point I had encountered God through avenues I had not learned in Christianity. I felt I had the ability to see God in everyone and everywhere, and I feared forming a more robust Christianity would rob me of that precious gift (that fear should give you an idea of the skewed view of Christianity I still held at the time). Even with a newly reclaimed love for Jesus I was suspicious of Christianity, because I did not feel represented by much of what was claimed to be fundamental to the faith.

Still, I felt in my soul a calling to go further along than where I was. Times of diving into the mystery are rich and comforting, but I learned that is not where God leaves us on our journey. Some people never move from deconstruction to reconstruction, but Jesus doesn't just destroy the temple, he reveals that he himself is the temple, which is to say it's not enough to tear down religious constructs that don't work, we have to do our due diligence to live in pursuit of the holy. Being an iconoclast is a terrible way to heal your soul or the world. While I hope I will always stand breathless before the Mystery, the Christian journey is not merely one of thinking rightly about these things. It is easy to get stuck in believing right thinking matters most. Wherever we are on the spectrum, from conservative fundamentalist to liberal progressive, we are easily fooled into believing the ways in which we achieve intellectual assent are more important than how we live our lives. This worship of doctrine stands in the way of worshiping Jesus, as all idolatry does. If our doctrine prevents us from going to uncomfortable places, loving uncomfortable people, and working with those who are different from you, our doctrine does not represent Christ very well. When you decide to follow Jesus, you enter into a big family that includes lots of people you'd rather not associate with. A true mark of enlightenment (or sanctification) is one's ability to maintain the tension of unity without needing uniformity.

When the Christian walk is exclusively about our ideas and doctrine it is all too easy to vilify anyone who disagrees with us, even if they also carry the designation of Christian. When the Christian walk is focused on living a just and generous life rather than on being God's defenders (as if the Creator of the universe needs defending), all of a sudden unity in the body of Christ matters because Christ left us with a hefty to-do list. We need each other and even our differences to properly advance God's beloved community on the earth. This is not to say theology and doctrine are not important. On the contrary, they are significant and necessary components of the Christian walk. Proverbs 27:19 tells us, "As the water reflects the face, so one's life reflects the heart." How we think impacts how we live. The fruit of our lives testifies to what we actually believe. However, when one steps back and watches the theological defenders at work, what one sees on both sides is agreement on at least one thing: the theological boxes one checks matter more than how one lives.

Naturally, my broadened appreciation for the mysteries of my faith created in me a stark criticism toward people who reminded me of my own arrogant and judgmental ways of perceiving God. I did not know it at the time, but even with a reconstructed understanding of Christianity, I had, again, gotten myself stuck in the idolization of my ideas. I was still an arrogant bully. How people thought about these things mattered to me so much more than how they lived their lives. It's amazing how convenient it is to ignore the final prayers of Christ in the garden when you think all that counts is what you believe. But Jesus didn't say this for nothing: "May they experience such perfect unity that the world will know that you sent me and that you love them as much as you love me" (John 17:23b NLT).

When I was young and conservative I loved to proof-text 1 Timothy 4:16 as an excuse to dismiss the ones I deemed theologically astray. In the passage Paul charges the young pastor to "Watch your life and doctrine closely . . . because if you do you will save yourself and your hearers." I would proudly cite the passage while ignoring how Jesus defined perfect doctrine in Matthew 22:37–39 as love for God and neighbor (or as love for God expressed through love of neighbor). When we pledge allegiance to a tribe because it's conservative or progressive we have neutered the gospel. It's just easier to call the Trump-supporting, young-Earth creationist digressive than it is to partner with him/her in the redemptive movements of the Spirit. It's easier to dismiss the Bernie Sanders-loving, theological liberal as a heretic than it is to work with them in advancing human flourishing on every level. We are content to use the aforementioned arguments as excuses to avoid each other. We fight, argue, and bludgeon each other over the head with out-of-context Bible verses, and all the while we testify something ugly to the world about God.

Transcend

It is remarkable how someone can shift their theology and ideology so much yet will still remain the same type of person. My opinions had undergone radical transition but my heart was still the same. More concerned with the party label than with the person, with correct theology than with character, and more likely to "other" those who disagreed with me. This realization hit me like a ton of bricks one day while I was spending time with my in-laws. My in-laws are not-so-secret conservative Christians. We did not always have the easiest time understanding each other during my times of doubt and deconstruction. They stood by principles and ideas I once intensely reinforced, but as I changed my outlook they did not. This was cause for a few uncomfortable conversations.

The thought pierced to me core one evening as Kelsey and I were spending the holidays with her folks and mine together. I observed how when I married Kelsey they did not just embrace me as their family, they embraced my dad and brother as family. After mom passed, and before I knew my in-laws, holidays felt broken, but because of their remarkable capacity for love we did not have broken holidays anymore. This thought hit like a ton of bricks: *my family, in-lawed and biological, are better people than I am.* Kelsey's family has stood by each other through more curve balls than just about any family I know. When they found out about my sexuality they embraced me as a son/brother. They let me cry on their shoulders, they affirmed me, and told me they loved me. When I asked uncomfortable questions, and raged against the machine, they were consistent with their love. I don't know that I have met a family with bigger hearts.

This thought led me to recall the moment I came out to my dad. I sat across from him at a crummy chain diner, more terrified than I can remember ever being. I had just been relieved from my position in the church he was attending, and no lie would suffice here. He had to know why. I needed to be my courageous and wholehearted self. So, I looked at my dad and began to speak with a quaking voice. I told him about my sexuality and about how scared it made me to realize getting married did not inhibit my ability to find other people attractive. I apologized and told him I would try anything to change. My dad stared at me with eyes full of compassion and sorrow. This strong pillar of protective love told me how sorry he was that our home was not a safer place for me growing up. He did not respond with anger or rejection, he responded in repentance.

PART II: A FAITH WORTH PASSING DOWN

I learned more about love, generosity, and service from my dad and in-laws than I ever could from a book or podcast. There was no policy or doctrine that could better demonstrate the power of love than what they had shown me. Yes, they voted and read the Bible differently than I did, and they stood by things I railed against, but their capacity for love was stronger than mine . . . and because of my dogmatic tribalism, as progressive as I pretended it was, I was missing out on the priceless gift it was just to be a part of this family. This sobering realization was cause for a course correction in my soul. I would allow myself to reject and scrutinize issues I found incongruent with following Jesus, but I never wanted to reject or scrutinize my family.

I learned a lot about the landscape of politics and theology with this humbling realization. The reactive person is not the rooted person. It does not matter whether you consider yourself conservative or progressive, if maintaining tribal boundaries is what's most important to you you will assuredly come across data that does not already confirm your bias or reinforce your ideals, your brain will sense fear, and you will either fight or flight. God is in the business of building oak trees, not peapods. Peapods grow quickly, only taking a few weeks before they reach maturation. Yet once fully grown it does not take much to knock them over. Oak trees take twenty to thirty years before they can even produce acorns, sometimes longer. But when an oak tree is fully grown it takes quite a bit of effort and skill to knock it over. Being a person who is so easily triggered by political and theological differences does not testify of a person rooted and secure in their walk with Christ. Someone rooted, confident, secure, and connected with the Spirit will be able to learn from people who think differently than them. God has not given us a Spirit of fear, so if we are always threatened by the "other" we are not being energized by God's Spirit.

I am not saying this to shame the person suffering from spiritual trauma into engaging in dialogue before they are ready. For a long time, I could not have these discussions without losing my cool, and that was indicative of the fact I was not ready to have these conversations. For some people, there is too much pain, abuse, oppression, rejection, and suppression wrapped up in certain religious topics to talk calmly about it with somebody who reinforces those triggers. That's okay. Take your space. Talk with safe people. Tribes are great places for healing. Just don't get suckered into throwing back the stones that were thrown at you.

Jesus transcended the idea of only embracing people totally in your camp. If I'm processing life and data in terms of "Does this best reflect *my side?*" I miss out on the transcendent power of Holy Spirit. It is the Unholy Spirit that causes me to dismiss beautiful people because I don't like how they vote or interpret Scripture. Not all political opinions are equally valid, and I definitely don't believe all ways of reading Scripture are equally healthy or coherent. I wholeheartedly endorse the quote commonly attributed to James Baldwin, which asserts, "We can agree to disagree unless your disagreement is rooted in my oppression and denial of my humanity," but I do believe in the inherit dignity and beauty of humanity. I believe every human being is made in the *imago Dei* and is of immeasurable value. It has been said we are truly free if we don't need people to be like us (in our religion, race, sexuality) before we can love them. It was a sobering realization that my progressivism did not make me more like Jesus. I was reactive, I wasn't rooted. I was progressive, but I was not making progress toward my deeper humanity, or toward what it meant to truly be part of the Jesus Movement. My progressivism had become its own kind of fundamentalism and often times came close to losing the Jesus of the Christian tradition.

Again, I found I was not actually pledging allegiance to Jesus, but to another human ideology. Being progressive for the sake of being progressive is not the same thing as being Christian, not any more than being conservative is the same thing as being Christian. Sometimes progressivism seems to reinvent (or reintroduce) Jesus in its own progressive image. It is undeniable that Jesus was significantly more progressive than the American church has made him out to be, but he did not come to be the mascot of American progressives any more than he did for the conservatives. Maybe this abandonment of biblical expression is just giving new language to the same ideas. Maybe the old way of talking about the kingdom of God and the new humanity carries with it too much baggage and trauma for people in order for it to have a meaningful impact. Maybe. But I'm not ready to lose thousands of years of world-healing, revelatory language to a few hundred years of exclusivism and destructive tribalism. I'm not ready to surrender the words of Christ or the ancient creeds of the church. I am not ready to throw in the towel and let American fundamentalism lay claim over the language of Scripture. If I believe this is the most beautiful story ever told, and that it is good news for all people in all places at all times, then I'm going to contend for the expressions that gave birth to such a movement.

At the end of the day, the church prioritizing political affiliation over discipleship does not work. It is not possible to do this without leaving dysfunction in your wake. This does not mean churches shouldn't speak to pertinent issues. On the contrary, the church must speak to the pressing issues of our time. But we drop the ball if we address the world as conservative or as progressive, *us* and *them*. The kingdom of God is not one of Republican or Democrat, progressive or conservative; it is a kingdom of *one new humanity* as Saint Paul so eloquently wrote in Ephesians 2. There is no room for *us* and *them* in one new humanity; we need a reconstructed vision of how the church relates to the empire that is the United States.

The Government of God

So, what is the proper Christian perspective here? Should Christians vote Republican? Should they vote Democrat? Should Christians vote at all? I'm not even going to begin to be able to settle the debate. I am sympathetic to the Anabaptist conviction which says Christians cannot endorse a politician without compromising their morals on some level. The 2016 election made this clear. Whether it was one candidate deceitfully deleting emails or another bragging about sexually assaulting women, many felt they had blood on their hands no matter who they voted for. Many from the Anabaptist movement, which has always sort of been a punk-rock expression of Christianity, would tell you it's not worth it to compromise the witness of the church by endorsing any politician, and we should refrain from voting at all. Let the world sort out the world's problems, the church needs to focus her energies on being the hands and feet of Jesus on the earth.

While I see the benefits of taking such a stance, that is not the one I'm advocating for here. However, the fact that there was ever a point where I could not see my faith outside of my politics is a tragedy. It is a tragedy because if you have ever seriously read Jesus, you know if he came and ran for president he would not win the Republican Party nomination, and he does not fit into the Democrat mold either. Jesus did not come to empower political parties and divide people with partisanship. Jesus cannot be claimed by any one political movement because he came with his own agenda. He came to establish his own government. So, when myself or any other Christian gets cut-throat and disparaging over a political candidate, well, I think we have on our hands a classic case of missing the point.

This is not to say Christians ought to remain totally unpolitical. The Gospels are littered with political subtext. Many of the titles that are ascribed to Jesus in the New Testament would have been ascribed to the emperor of Rome. Citizens of Rome would have had to confess with their mouths, "Caesar is lord." Caesar would have also been referred to as "the son of god" and "the prince of peace." Do any of those titles sound familiar? Jesus came and essentially subverted the nicknames of Caesar to make a dangerous, glorious, beautiful, and *political* point: he came to bring about a new kind of government. He did not come to empower Rome. He did not come to campaign for Caesar or one of Caesar's opponents. Jesus came to establish the only form of government that could bring about human flourishing on every level, beloved community in the kingdom of God. Jesus was not crucified because he made some ethereal promises about heaven and the afterlife, Jesus was executed by the state because he was viewed as a radical and political threat. He was a threat to the religious and political elite of their time who sought to benefit off of people's subordination.

> It stands to reason that Jesus is not interested in being used as a political mascot because he has his own political agenda.

It stands to reason that Jesus is not interested in being used as a political mascot because he has his own political agenda. Maybe referring to Jesus as King is too dated of a term for us to truly understand its implications, so let's borrow Shane Claiborne's book title and call Jesus *President*. If we are confessing with our mouths that Jesus is Lord that means we have no right to pledge allegiance to anything other than him. Our service, our loyalty, our time, our money, and our effort should go into the loving service of Christ and his good, peaceable kingdom. Jesus came to establish the kingdom of heaven *here and now*, a countercultural, present reality so effective in its work it should be a threat to existing power structures everywhere.

Barack Obama campaigned with his now-iconic tagline "Hope and change we can believe in." Many Christian progressives showed up in droves to support him, but the hope and change he sought to bring was never going to be as impactful as the hope and change we can bring if we come under the presidency of Jesus. Donald Trump, of course, borrowed Ronald Reagan slogans like "Make America great again" and "America first." There is nothing in Scripture or church tradition that could lead us to believe Jesus cares at all about America's greatness. And America first? Can

PART II: A FAITH WORTH PASSING DOWN

you imagine ancient Christians chanting "Rome first"?" There is no way; it would have been condemned as idolatry. Do political candidates have to accurately represent Jesus and the kingdom of God? Well, if they claim to be Christians, then yes! Though, most of us have given up on finding a candidate who does this. You can (and probably do) have reasons for supporting your party that has nothing to do with the kingdom of God, it would do us well to admit that (and then consider how appropriate it is that we would need something in a candidate that has nothing to do with the kingdom of God). Overspiritualizing politics is damaging. It misrepresents Jesus and it disenfranchises whoever is not in your political tribe.

In his book, *Subversive Sabbath*, A. J. Swoboda writes, "There is nothing healthy about being well-adjusted to a sick society." In the past, the church has acquiesced to the Religious Right at the expense of her witness to the world. We would be naïve to believe that doing a 180 in our direction and acquiescing to the Left will produce different results. In Scripture and in history the church has always thrived when it swam upstream and lived counter to the culture. The church has more options than to simply be a Christ-leaning religion which mirrors the culture.

To put it plain and simple: sacrificing Christian convictions to endorse a political candidate is idolatry. If we want to call ourselves Christians we have to be willing to bring ourselves under the presidency of Jesus. When I felt I was grasping at straws to try and make sense of my dwindling faith people would often tell me I needed to put my faith in God, not in people. Yet the books and sermons I ate up all pointed me to put my faith in their biblical interpretation, their moralizing, and their conservative hope for America. What do you do when the people who are supposed to be pointing you toward Christ are pointing you toward a worldview that does not work for you anymore?

Many, understandably, decide there is nothing more to the Jesus story than greed, violence, and power-mongering. If we want to see people in our churches and in Christian discipleship, we have to hand down a more Christlike praxis. We do not look to America to be the best great hope of the world, we look to Jesus and how he rallies his church. We do not look to a president to bring order out of the chaos in our world, we mobilize the church by taking the teachings of Jesus seriously. We do not work to make America great again under the ol' stars and stripes, we move to make Creation *shalom again*, as it was in the garden, under the banner of heaven. We must be cautious that our casting of votes to the Elephant or the Donkey does not prevent us from faithfully following the Lamb.

In Exile

So, what does this mean for the Christian? Does this mean the only way for a Christian to keep their hands clean is to abstain from politics altogether? Not so fast. As I previously mentioned, the Anabaptist position makes sense to me, and I don't fault whoever chooses that route, but I still believe there are things that need to be done which are beneficial to the kingdom of God that can most effectively be done through politics. We are called to neighborly love, and policies have the ability to effect of our neighbors on a macro level. Sometimes the most loving thing we can do is vote on policies that show the most love to people. You cannot tell me it didn't benefit the kingdom of God to abolish slavery, a necessary step made through politics. Without politics women would not be viewed as co-laborers as they were in the garden, and black Americans would still be lynched in the segregated Jim Crow South.

Jeremiah 29:7 reads, "Seek the peace and prosperity of the city to which I have carried you into exile. Pray to the LORD for it, because if it prospers, you too will prosper." This was the prophet Jeremiah's instructions to Israel after seeing his country destroyed, and his people being carried off to Babylon. It is difficult to overstate how devastating the effects of seeing their country laid to waste would have had on the nation. Not only was this the land promised to them through Abraham, it was the land they believed the Lord had delivered to them through the conquests of Joshua. But the most devastating blow delivered would have been the destruction of the temple, the very heart of the city. The temple was built to host the Presence of God. We do not have anything in our country that can be considered as sacred as the temple would have been to Israel, not even the White House. To see its destruction was to call into question their entire history with YHWH. Watching the temple destroyed could have been taken as a sign that God either was not all-powerful, had abandoned his people, or never existed in the first place.

Bearing this in mind makes Jeremiah's instruction to the exiled nation to seek the peace and prosperity of their enemies all the more controversial. Israel would have had two dominant temptations and courses of action during this period: the first was to bend and become like Babylon. Many would have abandoned their customs, religion, and heritage to adopt the Babylonian way and seek positions of privilege within the new country. The other temptation would have been to try and destroy Babylon. They would hang on to their anger and hatred, and seek any opportunity to revolt against their captors. Both of these courses of action are easy to sympathize with, but God called them to a third way: seek good for Babylon, but never surrender their heritage and true loyalty to YHWH. They were called to live in the tension of loyalty and subversion. We see this modeled beautifully in the story of Daniel, the Israelite prophet who rises through the ranks in Babylon, but never betrays his truest loyalty to the God of Israel.

This tension of loyalty and subversion has become the standard for God's people from Babylonian captivity until he comes to reclaim creation. In the Bible, Babylon would come to symbolize any empire that rose to power and demanded allegiance from God's people. Egypt, Persia, and Rome are all types of Babylon in Scripture (bear that in mind the next time you read the book of Revelation). The Bible Project, which is is the best ecumenical resource I'm aware of, is a YouTube channel dedicated to bringing the Scriptures to life. In their "Way of the Exile" video, they tell us "Babylon becomes a symbol for any human institution that demands allegiance to its idolatrous redefinitions of good and evil . . . we all live and work in Babylon."

As the children of God there is a responsibility for us to seek ways to bring prosperity to the places we have been sent to. We have a mandate to serve, love, and improve wherever we are. Politics are sometimes the most efficient way to accomplish this, but we have to approach this as people carried into exile. We are to approach our country, not as our permanent residence, but as the place we temporarily live in. We are strangers and exiles in a foreign land, and we cannot live as though this is our home. We wait, work, worship, love, serve, laugh, suffer, and celebrate as citizens of God's beloved community exiled in Babylon, working to build a countercultural reality within our context. Remember we are building an eternal kingdom, not America, which is the type of kingdom moth and rust will destroy.

How then should we vote as followers of Jesus? How do we live in the government of God while casting votes in the government of man? For me, the answer is not that difficult. Jesus is my president, and everything I do should be a reflection of this reality. I don't want there to be a single aspect of my life that appears to be out of step with Jesus. And though this journey of Christlikeness will surely be a lifelong pursuit where I stumble my way through, I know enough to know if I claim to follow Jesus, I should at least vote like someone who does. Read the Sermon on the Mount and Matthew 25, and when voting, ask yourself: Is it good for the hungry? Is it good for the stranger (or foreigner or immigrant)? Is it good for the poor? Is it good for the sick? Is it good for the prisoner? Is it good for the orphan or the widow? But maybe the most important question we need to ask as we vote is this: Does my vote reflect and reveal the love and character of Jesus?

*For more on living and working in Babylon, Pastor Brian Zahnd wrote a fantastic book called *Postcards from Babylon*, check it out.

CHAPTER ELEVEN

The Jesus of Suburbia is a Lie

> "We must learn that to passively accept an unjust system is to cooperate with that system, and become a participant in its evil."
> —DR. MARTIN LUTHER KING JR.

> "What does the Lord require of you but to do justice, love mercy, and walk humbly with your God?"
> —MICAH 6:8 (NIV)

Here and Now

IT IS WORTH MENTIONING again that people are not leaving churches or questioning their faith because their religion is too much like Jesus. On the contrary, much of the mass exodus churches have been seeing in recent years is because our faith does not look enough like Jesus. If churches want to offer anything of significance to the world they would do well not to stray from embodying the way of Christ. The world does not need more overspiritualized political movements, greedy bait-and-switches, or another social club. The world needs what it has always needed: Jesus. The world needs beloved communities that embody peace, forgiveness, justice, generosity, obedience, inclusivity, faithfulness, and concern for the ones on the margins.

For many there is a feeling of passivity in the church. Some sense there is almost an unwillingness to go all in to bring healing into the world. I believe this stems from many people practicing a faith that tells them very little of what they do in this life matters. Many people believe the only choice of eternal consequence they will make is whether or not they pray a prayer of salvation. For many, Christianity is simply biding our time and sinning as little as possible on earth until we can get to heaven. This idea finds its roots more in the philosophy of Plato and the pagan gnostic religion than it does in biblical and historic Christianity.

Gnosticism was condemned as heresy by the early church. Gnosticism contends that all material matter is ruled by a lesser divinity, and Christ came to liberate the human spirit from the prisons of their earthly bodies. This flies in the face of God breathing his Spirit into the nostrils of humanity, giving life to the marriage of the material and the Divine. We are breathed-upon dirt, part of creation and not separate from it. Jesus taught his followers to pray for the will and kingdom of God to come on earth as it is in heaven (Matt 6:10). Elsewhere, Jesus tells his listeners the kingdom of God is "*among you*" (Luke 17:21). Saying God saved us so we can wait until we die and go to heaven is like God buying car insurance for a car that doesn't drive. Humanity still longs for the coming of Christ, and unfortunately many have found the church to be lacking in demonstrating good news through our love and justice.

There was once a time where the church was known for its scandalous love, radical service, and vision for societal innovation. Schools, hospitals, orphanages, and social work all find their origins on the backs of faithful Christ-followers. Jesus did not merely tell us about the kingdom of heaven, he showed it to us and invited us to participate in it. We see this in the ways Jesus brought healing everywhere he went. He brought healing by resurrecting the dead, forgiving the unforgivable, eating meals with the ones pushed to the edges of society, praising the faith of folks from other religions, and demonstrating a God who is for all people. Jesus showed us what God looks like, and that's some good news!

Many communities of faith have done beautiful jobs incarnating the heavenly reality in our world today, much more than society gives the church credit for. Indeed, more than this book is giving it credit for. However, there is still much more that needs to be done. Today if you ask the average American person, middle-aged and younger, they will tell you church by and large is better known for her ugly and damaging history than for her Christlikeness. You'll hear words like "Crusades," "hypocrisy," "homophobia," "misogyny," "racism," and "scandals." The world is running out

PART II: A FAITH WORTH PASSING DOWN

of patience for communities of faith who don't offer anymore than spiritual fire insurance (please know I do not say this with any intention to downplay the cosmic salvific work Christ accomplished). The world needs a church that looks like Christ's body. Many understandably look at the chaos and carnage in our world and they feel hopelessness and despair. The good news is there's a solution, and that solution is you, me, the church. If we want to live like the beloved community of God, we have to live here and now, and that means we have to be aware of what takes place in our time and space.

The Side of the Crucified Ones

My first job out of high school, in addition to interning at my church, was at a soul food BBQ restaurant. The owners had moved to Oregon in an attempt to franchise the successful business they managed in Las Vegas. This was down-South-inspired soul food, with recipes passed down through the generations of the owners. Walking in the restaurant at 11:00 AM every morning was to be met with the smells of smoked pulled pork, fresh baked corn bread, peach cobbler, and homemade mac 'n' cheese. It was my first job, but it was also my first close-up exposure to African-American culture. I had a few black friends growing up, but we occupied dominantly white spaces. So, rather than learning about the experience of my black friends, they acquiesced to fit into mine and that of my peers. However, every day going to work was me stepping out of my comfort zone and into theirs. Mamma C was one of the owners, a lady who exuded kindness, generosity, and love. Her husband, Henry, was a cranky, no-nonsense man who found his own ways to demonstrate empathy. Working alongside them were Henry's brother and sister in-law, their son, and his girlfriend—all African-American. It was the first time I realized how segregated my life really was. I never thought of the world I grew up in as a white world, but seeing the subculture my employers occupied showed me just how foolish I was.

Everyday going to work was like stepping into a different world. I came from Fox News, but playing on the television daily at work was MSNBC. I looked forward to the new Seth Rogen movies, but they made it an event whenever a new Tyler Perry movie came out. We closed the store during Whitney Houston's funeral out of respect, and when Obama won his second term they threw a party. When Trayvon Martin was murdered and George Zimmerman was acquitted, the family wept, but my news stations told me justice was served. One afternoon I was cleaning the counters and tables of the little restaurant when the son of the family told me he wondered if Trayvon's dad gave him the same talk his own father gave him.

"The talk?" I asked.

He proceeded to tell me about the talk his father gave him when he received his driver's license. He told me most black people get "the talk." His father told him, "Son, when you get pulled over, it doesn't matter whether or not you think you did anything wrong, you keep your hands where the officer can see them at all times. You don't reach for anything unless the officer gives you direct permission, and even if he does, move slowly. You always respond with, 'Yes, sir,' or 'No, sir.' You have to prove you aren't going to pull a gun on them."

My friend continued.

"Now, I know Trayvon wasn't killed by a cop, but all of me and my friends grew up understanding that when an adult in a rich neighborhood tells you to do anything, it doesn't matter what it is, you do it because the color of your skin means you always look like a threat."

In my ignorance, I asked him why his dad gave him this talk. I never had this talk, and I never heard of my friends getting it either. He laughed a full-bellied laugh at my ignorance, and then responded, "Because some folks are just trigger-happy when it comes to black people. We've lost friends and family because they were reaching for their license and the officer assumed they were reaching for a gun."

I'm sure there's more to it than that, I thought. *This is a little melodramatic.*

I kept my opinions to myself. I knew better than to argue with him.

I was conditioned to believe if a cop shot somebody, it was not because of the color of their skin, it was because the person they shot was a perceived threat. It was that simple for me. In the following siege of unarmed black folks getting shot by police, with all the cell phone footage of it taking place, I trusted conservative pundits to form the narrative for me about why this was happening. In the wake of the deaths of Eric Garner, Michael Brown, and many others, I tried to remain unfazed, trusting the voices I heard on the news stations I watched. But all that changed just a few weeks before I got married, years after I had left the BBQ restaurant.

On the afternoon of November 23rd, 2014, in Cleveland, officers Timothy Loehmann and Frank Garmback received a call from a 9-1-1 dispatcher informing them there was a black male at the local recreation center with a gun. As the officers pulled up to the recreation center they

PART II: A FAITH WORTH PASSING DOWN

saw the gun sitting on the table, the person picked the gun up and put it in his waistband. Officer Loehmann called for the gentleman to raise his hands. Instead, the young man put his hands on the handle of the gun. Officer Loehmann fired two shots, hitting him in the torso once. He died the following day.

The black guy was a twelve-year-old boy named Tamir Rice. The gun was an airsoft gun with an orange tip, signaling it was a nonlethal weapon. It's hard to imagine any reason Tamir reached for the gun other than to show the orange tip. The caller told the dispatcher multiple times, "the gun looks fake." This dispatcher asked the caller multiple times if the kid with the gun was white or black. They failed to inform the officers the caller repeatedly told them the gun was probably fake . . . . Yet made sure the cops new Tamir was black. Next, a twelve-year-old kid laid there on the ground with a gunshot wound in the torso and a toy in his hand.

At the time of this shooting I was a middle school pastor with a few kids of color in my youth group. I could not shake the image of one of them getting shot for playing with a toy, or getting the cops called on them for it in the first place. I can't tell you how many times my friends and I played with toy guns in parks or in our front lawns where anybody could see us. We even went as far as coloring in the orange tips so the guns looked real. No one ever called the cops on us.

This led me to confront a real darkness within myself and country. When a white kid played with a toy gun I thought of my brother, friends, and myself. When a black kid had a toy gun I thought of gang affiliation. I thought I despised racism and opposed it. I thought my country moved beyond it. I was horrified to discover not only had I benefited from societal racism, I contributed to it. Even if I would never call a black person the N-word, I immediately excused and defended the repeated killing of unarmed black folks. I revisited the footage of Eric Garner's death, and wept as he continued to gasp out the words "I can't breathe" while he was being choked to death. I wept because of the injustice of it. I wept because I defended it. I don't say this to virtue signal to anyone; I say it to convey the sadness and shame I felt.

Why was all of this happening? Because the pernicious beast of racism is alive and well. It may not be socially kosher to spout racial epithets at people, but racism is a sneakier, subtler monster than that.

Michael Brown, Eric Garner, Philando Castile, Emerson Clayton, Emantic Fitzgerald Bradford, Jimmy Atchison, and literally hundreds more in the last decade, all unarmed black folks killed by police. That's not to mention unarmed black people murdered by people abusing their second amendment right, like Trayvon Martin and Jordan Davis.

After Tamir Rice, all of a sudden my friend from the restaurant did not seem so melodramatic. Shortly after Tamir's murder it was revealed that officer Loehmann had been fired from his previous police job because he was deemed emotionally unstable and unfit for service. Later, Loehmann would lose his job for withholding that information from the police. Today, as of writing this, Loehmann has been hired back.

Why am I bringing race into this? Isn't this a book about faith transitions and the church? That is precisely why I bring it up. The Christian worldview I clung to did not have much to say to the disproportionate number of unarmed black people who were killed by the police. My worldview did not offer anything to the epidemic of mass incarceration for people of color. According to the U.S. Bureau of Justice Statistics as of April 2019, white folks make up 58 percent of the American prison population, while black people make up 38 percent. When you factor in the fact that African Americans barely make up more than 12 percent of the American population as whole, these numbers become astounding. It should jolt us into attention and force us to ask, "What, on a systemic and structural level, is taking place where a disproportionate amount of African-Americans are being incarcerated?" Recent statistics are reporting that one out of every three black people will be arrested. Why? You can't say it's because black people are genetically predisposed to committing crimes—that is the same sadistic rhetoric white folks used during slavery. It's not as simple as prejudice, the evils that keep people of color on the margins of society are bigger than individual prejudices. The reason is systemic racism. Our society is still structured in such a way where being a person of color puts you at a severe disadvantage.

The truth is I did not see this earlier because I did not want to see it earlier. My theology was comprised of eternal fire insurance, the sovereignty of God, speaking in tongues, and some shady atonement theories . . . I did not have to formulate a here-and-now theology because I was privileged enough to place my hope in going some other place at some other time when I died. A Christianity that is all ideas, equations, philosophies, and post-mortem hope is not Christianity at all. Suburban, upper-class people can embrace this false gospel and pass it along to middle- and lower-class folks because there is no realization of the need for an aggressive confrontation of brokenness in our world. If you are wronged, you hire a lawyer. If your marriage is falling apart, you go to marriage counseling. If you're depressed, you take anti-depressants. If you feel your kid is being mistreated at school, you complain to a teacher or administrator. I'm not knocking any of these things. I have taken medication for depression. I go to counseling. I'm just pointing out resources people of privilege have that those on the margins do not have. These are needs the church can meet.

Not only does a disembodied faith not represent Jesus accurately, it has been the cause of many coming to the conclusion that Christianity has nothing to offer the world anymore. Quite frankly, there is a growing number of disenfranchised folks who have no patience for faith practices that don't raise some noise in our world today. Unfortunately for many evangelical churches, inaction is a best-case scenario. Recently, Reformed superstar pastor John MacArthur has spoken out against a Christian concern for social justice, only cementing in many people's minds Christianity as an antiquated philosophy. MacArthur seems to ignore the fact that God is on the side of the crucified ones. We would do well to pay heed to Jonathan Martin's words on social media when he said, "If we hand our sons and daughters a faith exposed as misogynistic, racist, unconcerned about creation and the poor, they aren't wrong to leave it." Any honest reading of the Gospels will show you that a Christlike life is impossible without love and concern for the ones on the margins, and not only love and concern for them, but advocacy for and elevation of them, not so we can pat ourselves on the back and become self-praising virtue-signalers, but so we can do what we can to partner with people to become liberators in their own narratives. It is unimaginable for one to consider Christ their king and show no concern for the ones he spent the majority of his time with.

It is through Pistis You Have Been Saved

When I was seventeen and new to the faith, I had a dream someone I loved had been sent to hell. I remember in the dream seeing him wander around this desert, screaming and begging for just a drop of water. In this dream, he found a cactus and when he eagerly broke it open in an attempt to get water, only dust poured out. I woke up in tears. I felt it was my mission to prevent that from happening to as many people as possible. My goal was not necessarily discipleship or to teach the way of Jesus, my goal was to save my peers from torment in hell. When this is your mission, you feel permission to forsake kindness for rightness—after all, souls are on the line. It's sad to think that in my understanding of the Gospel at the time I saw a difference between the way of Jesus and one being saved from hell. As I have deconstructed and reconstructed my faith over the years I have learned taking up the way of Jesus for yourself is the central piece of what makes the story of Christ good news. The idea that the Gospel is simply Jesus dying for your sins so you don't to go to hell is so anemic it's borderline offensive. To insist on that formula being the complete Gospel is also unbiblical.

When I was working my tail off as a junior in high school for the souls of my peers, a verse I would often cite to them was Ephesians 2:8, which reads "For it is by grace you have been saved, through faith." Grace through faith. God has given you the grace of offering forgiveness, you just have to have faith in him. Think the right thing, pray the magic words, and your soul will be saved forever. My gospel formula did not know what to do with the life and teachings of Jesus, he was only useful to me because of his death on the cross. Even his resurrection was only something I made a big deal of because the apostle Paul did. I didn't know why I needed Jesus to resurrect, I just knew I needed him to die in my place. This way of thinking came from learning to apply the writings of Paul above the accounts of Christ in the Gospels. Of course, no one told me explicitly to do this, but it was modeled in the way I saw Christianity practiced and defended. This is inevitable when you teach people a flat reading of Scripture which insists every word is equally authoritative for today. Paul's arguments were systematic, they were reasonable (for the most part), and they were well-articulated. Jesus, the radical, enemy-loving rabbi who only had a church with attendance of 120 when he ascended, is a much riskier master to follow.

Over the years I have learned if one ever feels that applying the writings of Paul creates tension with the accounts of Jesus, one must always pick Jesus, and then reconsider how they're reading Paul. Jesus is Lord, not Paul. Jesus is King, not Paul. Jesus lived the life of the prototype human, not Paul. Jesus was sinless, Paul was not. Jesus died and rose again, disarming death and ushering in the new reality of resurrection, not Paul. The writings of Paul are inspired, beautiful, and compelling literature every Christian should be familiar with, but they are always to be subordinate to Jesus. I had been a Christian for most of my life by the time I deconstructed, but I was not very Christlike. I was a great disciple of someone based on Paul, but a poor disciple of Jesus. Not only would Jesus take umbrage with this, but I believe I would have received a rebuking from Paul himself over it. Placing the letters of Paul at the center of my faith made it easier for me to embrace a faith that was exclusive, arrogant, and safe.

In reality, Paul and Jesus are much more in tandem than it would seem at first glance. Let's look at Ephesians 2:8 again, where Paul tells us it is grace through *faith* that saves us. Elsewhere, in Romans 3:21–23, Paul tells us we can attain the righteousness of God on our behalf because of *faith* in Jesus. For much of my journey I believed this faith Paul is calling us toward was one of intellectual assent. Just put your *faith* in Christ's sacrifice for you and you will receive salvation. But when you visit this word "faith" in the original Greek for both of these sections of Scripture, new layers arrive for us to consider. The word here for "faith" in the original Greek is *pistis*. Pistis is a fun word because when you say it out loud it sounds like you're cussing, but it also is a deeply layered word. Pistis is often translated in our English Bibles as a type of faith which places confidence or trust in God. It is a belief that is not based on proof, and this is definitely one way of interpreting the word, but there is another interpretation that is far costlier. Pistis can also be translated as *faithfulness* or *fidelity*. Fidelity is a strict observance to a promise made.

I choose fidelity to my wife; I have promised to love, serve, and honor her for the rest of my life. In his book, *Salvation by Allegiance Alone*, professor Matthew Bates writes, "Properly speaking, Pistis is not part of the Gospel, but the only fitting response to the Gospel." The call to living connection with God is not simply one of acknowledging in our heads and hearts spiritual laws which lead to an after-death salvation. Jesus' call to his disciples is one in which we are instructed to clothe the poor, feed the hungry, welcome the foreigner, visit the prisoner, and comfort the sick (Matt 25:40). It is a call to love and bless your enemies (Matt 5:43-48), to take up your cross daily (Luke 9:23), to lose your life in order to find it (Matt 10:39), and to live as servants to the world (John 13, Phil 2). Pistis is not merely a call to faith, it is a call to faithfulness.

Becoming a Christian, being saved by faith, is not simply a matter of trust, it's a commitment to living life in your context as a healing presence in the world. It is both seeing all the ways in which *shalom* has been disrupted and restoring it. Following Jesus is a call to seek human flourishing on every level. Romans 10:9 says, "If you confess with your mouth that Jesus is Lord and believe in your heart that God raised him from the dead, you will be saved." Proclaiming Jesus as Lord is not a magic spell that changes the destination of your soul, it is a declaration of whose lordship

THE JESUS OF SUBURBIA IS A LIE

you are submitting your life to. Who is lord over your life? Is it American ideals? Your president? Your political party? Your fear of growing and learning? Your addiction to safety? Yourself? None of those things have proven to offer the ability to heal souls and redeem the world—only Jesus can do that.

To those who might dismiss me as promoting a works-based faith: I am not saying it is how we live which grants us access to eternal life. The resurrection of Christ attained that for us. But how we live directly reflects who or what we worship. We do violence to the Christian tradition if we continue to promote an expression of Christianity that leaves room for folks to sit in complicity with evil in our world and feel at peace about it because they confessed with their mouths that Jesus is Lord. We have to be willing to say if someone is content to sit back and watch things fall apart, and feels no responsibility to be a part of the solution, they are not really following Jesus. Our lives are a witness to the bigger story we have bought into. Following Jesus requires hard work, not work to build bigger church buildings, crowds, budgets, staffs, or influences in society. Those things can be great benefactors to the work of Christ, but they become corrupt when they aren't put to the use of benefitting the most vulnerable in society and revealing how to live as a beloved community. We don't work to be more progressive by cultural standards, we don't do it out of allegiance to a political party or social trend, we do this because when we heard the good news that Jesus is King something in our souls leaped with joy because we know if Jesus is King of the world, it is a good world, or at least it's going to be.

As of writing this chapter, a video was released of a young black man, Ahmaud Arbery, who was attacked and shot by a group of white men while on a jog, one an ex-cop. The footage of this modern-day lynching was released two months after his death, and it was two months before arrests were made. Just over a month later video footage was released of George Floyd, another unarmed black man, being murdered by police. As I finish the final touches to this chapter we are on the 8th consecutive night of protests in my city. Just a week ago, riots broke out all over the world in response to the murders. We are in a season of civil unrest unlike anything we have seen in my lifetime. There are so many fears, traumas, worries, and problems, and through all of this I grow ever more convinced Christ as revealed in beloved community is the solution.

May we have a clear vision for a mobilized church determined to bring the realities of heaven here and now. May we pass down to generations a faith which is so beneficial to society that the notion of deconstruction would seem ridiculous. The church gets hit with a lot of stones in our world today, and some of them she deserves. People are leaving, doubting, and rejecting the worldviews they were brought up with. But the soul knows when it spots good news, and churches can be conduits of that good news. We just have to be willing to be communities which incarnate heaven as Jesus did, and we must be unwilling to settle for less.

CHAPTER TWELVE

What is a Healthy Construct?

> "Jesus' central message was not primarily about how to get to heaven when you die, or about becoming a better person. The central message of Jesus was about the coming of God's kingdom."
> —PRESTON SPRINKLE

> "Seek first the kingdom of God."
> —MATTHEW 6:33 (NIV)

What are We Building?

I HAVE SPENT THE last eleven chapters breaking down and dissecting the ways in which my methods of engaging life, faith, and politics have changed. I feel it is important to point out I have refrained from trying to incriminate any personal friend, teacher, mentor, or pastor who may have unintentionally contributed to my deconstruction, because I am a particularly zealous person. I take a little guidance, instruction, and encouragement, and I run with it full speed ahead. They may have given an inch of teaching that needed to be deconstructed, but I took it to the extreme mile. The teachers in my life who taught me these things did so with the best of intentions, they were trying to build something in me. But either the thing they were trying to build or the intensity with which I received it needed to be torn down and rebuilt, and after all this tearing down we must ask the question: What are we building? We are not to be demolishers of philosophy; we are builders of God's kingdom. What does that look like? As a spiritual person, a Christian, and a leader in the church, this question pursues me. I want to be a part of building a people who faithfully model Christ to the world. I want to model truth-telling in calling out contaminated religion, and calling us forward to the simple way of Jesus.

There are many methods to embody the Jesus Way. You can do this in a church of 10,000 so long as the leadership never loses sight that their enlarged influence and budget do not make it easier to pursue the simple way; it makes it harder. You can do it in a home group of five so long as you know that resources and influence increase the church's capacity for radical generosity and contribution to the world. Whether you worship in a megachurch, a house church, or you're still deciding if you want to worship at all; whether you're in a mainline church with hymns and a homily, or a charismatic church with pop worship songs and a fifty-minute sermon, or some beautiful conglomeration of it all; whether you lean conservative, or progressive, or center, below are the things we need to pass down to the next generation. We have to answer the question: Who are we as a Jesus-centered community? This is not comprehensive, we all have things we wish we would have heard at our first coming to faith, but these are things I needed to hear, or did hear and did not respond to.

We are Clear about the Essentials

If you asked a twenty-two-year-old me what the final word and authority of my faith was, I would have told you the Bible. Today, my response would be slightly more nuanced than that. You see, this may come as a surprise to you, but the Bible is a big book. Not only that but it has at least thirty-five different authors, possibly more depending on whom you ask. These authors lived in different times and places. They were of varying backgrounds and financial statuses. So, because of the wonderful diversity of authorship when it comes to the Bible it should not be a surprise that the Bible has a number of things to say about any given topic. Does God desire mercy, or sacrifice? Does he want us to bless our enemies or wipe them out? Does God want to liberate slaves, or does he enable slavery? Does God want to release women into the ministry, or does he expect them to remain silent when men are in the room? Should husbands only have one wife, or is polygamy acceptable? Depending on where you read you can use the Bible to defend any one of these positions.

A pivotal piece in my deconstruction journey was my inability to find cohesion in the Scriptures. The whole Bible was the final authority on faith, which was like saying everything in it was an essential issue. But when we observe our Christian forefathers and mothers, we know this was not the case for them. Historically, the Apostle's Creed and the Nicene Creed have served as a comprehensive listing of what Christians have always found essential. When you consider everything essential, you are bound to make mountains out of molehills, or you are bound to consider nothing as essential; the negative implications of this are clear. Additionally, when you consider everything essential you are not given permission to disagree with people charitably. The truth is, as much as we want everything in the Bible to be equally authoritative in our faith, there is not a person alive who lives that way because it is impossible. When we do this, we are asking the Bible to do something it was not meant to do. We need clarity on what it means to be a Christian on a fundamental level.

I am not suggesting we switch from being biblical Christians to creedal Christians, nor am I saying the creeds are more God-breathed than the Bible. How could the contents of the creeds exist if they were not informed by the Scriptures? We will dive into how we read the Bible in a moment, but for now allow me to bring into focus what the Bible and church history have always endorsed as a sense of orthodoxy.

A friend of mine who is much smarter than I explained it this way: we ought to imagine three concentric circles. The very center of the first circle is where we would place the essentials. These are the bare minimum things you must endorse if you are to be considered an orthodox Christian. If we are allowing the creeds to inform what we consider essential or orthodox, this would include a belief in the Trinity, the resurrection, affirmation of the Lordship of Christ, and a few other things. In the next ring of the circle we would put things we consider to be *dogma*. Topics that are dogma are topics certain church communities heavily affirm and embrace, while acknowledging that if one does not endorse these things that does not mean one is not a Christian. It may be difficult to be in a church community whose dogma you do not agree with, but that does not mean you are not all under the massive tent of Christ's love. The third and final ring would be matters of opinion. These are issues we hold loosely. We may experience disagreements over these things, but there is a common understanding that we do not break fellowship or provoke outrage over these topics.

PART II: A FAITH WORTH PASSING DOWN

I cannot stress how important it is that we pass down a faith with these distinctions. Too many people have completely jumped ship who did not need to because they changed their views on evolution or questioned how to relate to their sexuality. Too many people have broken off relationships and sown discord into the body of Christ because they treated dogma or matters of opinion as essential. We have not given enough permission to disagree with one another. Without these distinctions, it is inevitable that we will pass down a faith that is caustic, inharmonious, arrogant, and impossible to live out faithfully. May we major in the majors.

We are Spiritual and Religious

A lot of folks who have undergone similar experiences as myself have opted out of church and organized religion altogether. While we are seeing an unprecedented decline in church attendance in America, that does not mean all or even most of the people leaving our churches are taking the deep-dive into atheism. More and more people every year are referring to themselves as spiritual but not religious. This means there is an outstanding level of openness to spiritual things for those who will not worship in the four walls of the church anymore. And you can understand why many choose this route. There is freedom to explore the Divine without the harsh rigidity many have experienced in church. It allows for new ways of experiencing God without feeling the need to apply too many definitions and rules to it. You can sit from a distance and scrutinize other faiths, and take for your own walk the things that work for you while disregarding the rest. Maybe for some it is a way of hanging on to God without having to be subjected to trauma they experienced in religious settings. For others, it might be a way to keep their souls alive after their faith communities have gone places politically and theologically they cannot follow. While I understand why one would opt in for the path of spiritual-but-not-religious, there are a few concerns I have with it.

The church world really was a pioneer for the "spiritual but not religious" movement when we started slinging the axiom, "Christianity is not a religion, it's a relationship." If you were involved in evangelical culture during the 2000s, you definitely heard some version of this. There is a good instinct here. I used to be one who offered such a platitude. The folks who seemed more legalistic than me were ones I called "religious," and it was always used as a slur. The instinct here is to emphasize the living connection

WHAT IS A HEALTHY CONSTRUCT?

we have with God as the central piece of our faith journey, not dogmas and rules that have been the crux of so many people's hurts. The problem is I was not less of a religious person than the ones I criticized, I was just religious in different ways, and not even always in less destructive ways. It is possible to lean into the healthy impulses of religion without feeling the need to disregard it altogether.

The truth is you are going to be hard pressed to find anyone who isn't religious about something. If you are a person who holds a set of beliefs concerning a cause and purpose, who holds some sort of ritualistic devotions with a moral code that governs your affairs, guess what? You're religious. You don't have to attend a church or subscribe to a faith system for that to be true of you. We should not strive to be spiritual without also being religious because that has proven to be a fool's errand. Rather, we should choose our religion cautiously. Religion tethers us to a set of practices which can be tremendously beneficial to ourselves and the world around us, or it can tether us to something traumatizing and harmful.

If we chose to abandon religion altogether we lose the wisdom of the past and a vision for the future. This is one of the great benefits of the Christian religion. Our sacred text and church practices are full of wisdom and vision. Partaking in the Eucharist causes us to remember the ways in which Christ was broken and given for the betterment of the world, and it also offers a vision for how the church is invited to go and do likewise. Human beings are storied creatures. As I've said before, all any of us are doing is trying to find the narrative that best makes sense of the world around us. Religion gives us a story, a context to live in. And if you are a part of the Christian religion we have such a rich past full of wisdom and the potential for a beautiful future full of hope. Religion-less Christianity has resulted in the troubling entanglement of the church with American ideals we spoke of earlier. Rather than making service to Christ our religion, we made it service to country. The two are not the same and are often mutually exclusive. Many evangelical churches today use the language of Christianity while worshipping empire, power, wealth, and protection. Christianity is a received faith with a King and a kingdom all its own; we don't get to make it up as we go.

This does not mean we shut down or suppress spiritual curiosity. Recently I had the privilege of speaking to a group of men from a variety of Alcoholics Anonymous groups who had asked various faith leaders to come and share who their higher power is and why. I gave my lecture right after a Buddhist Zen Master shared his beautiful story and offered rich practices. As I have mentioned, I am not into salad bar spirituality—I am a Christian—but Zen Master Hugh's words pierced my heart. I needed to implement his wisdom on meditation and love. His remarks have enriched my spiritual life. There is nothing wrong with spiritual curiosity, but if you are a follower of Jesus, that truth ought to anchor you and everything you do.

We are Being and Becoming

Religion, like deconstruction, can be a terrible or beautiful thing depending on how we approach it. When religion is so inflexible it does not have room to adapt to the ever-changing tides of culture, the best-case scenario is it loses its relevance, while the worst case is it destroys lives. Let us look at how the church has treated the LGBTQ+ community over the last fifty years. Regardless of your experience with or exposure to this community, there is no denying the church's unwillingness to grow and understand has come at the cost of thousands of LGBTQ+ lives. Preston Sprinkle is a writer and professor who has done extensive work on educating churches about the horrific ways in which this community has been mistreated in the church, while also doing extensive work on how churches can lovingly hold to what is being called the traditional view of marriage. In his book, *People to Be Loved*, Preston writes, "The church is supposed to be a hospital for the sick, not a museum for the saints . . . so, when did it become a graveyard for LGBT people?" The tide has been changing in more recent years, and more churches today than at any other point are grappling with the question of love and inclusion when it comes to this community, to varying degrees of success. But Preston's point still stands. Most studies show you are much more likely to attempt suicide if you are an LGBTQ+ person from a religious background than if you were born in a nonreligious family. That is religion gone bad.

Recently I was talking with a pastor who bragged to me about not having changed their views or theology in over thirty years. He believed it was a testament to his faithfulness. I understand this perspective, and I do believe there are essentials in Christianity that must be observed in order to still consider yourself a part of the historic Christian tradition. Jesus is the same today, yesterday, and forever, after all. However, if you haven't changed or adjusted your beliefs about faith and practice you can't

WHAT IS A HEALTHY CONSTRUCT?

really claim to be growing in your relationship with Christ. Whether you lean conservative or lean progressive, Christianity is at its ugliest when its members refuse to model teachability and humility. We are works in progress, ever so slowly inching our way toward Christlikeness. This is a lifelong journey that requires change and growth. If we want to pass down a faith that looks enough like Jesus that it won't require deconstruction, we have to pass down the virtue of being a lifelong learner.

Maybe God's beloved community includes the people you would have never associated with when you first came to faith. You might have Bible verses and books by reputable authors to prove they ought not be included, but maybe God is still in the business of catching us religious people off-guard by how expansive his love is. Maybe God has standards of behavior for his people you will have difficulty observing, but just because you don't like the standards or struggle to honor them does not mean they aren't there. Maybe what God expects for one person is not the same for the whole collective, because God sees us in our personal contexts and knows what's best for each of us. This isn't moral relativism, it's the grace of God leading us in ways that will bring about the most fruit. Maybe Jesus really meant it when he said judge not or you too will be judged (Matt 7:1 NIV). The point is, God is not interested in fitting into the boxes we try to put God in. The only time you will find God in a box is because he wants to be where we are. God is wildly free, infinitely mysterious, and loving beyond our wildest dreams. A thousand lifetimes are not enough to learn all there is to know about the Divine.

May we have awareness that we are all works in progress. The thing God is doing in you will not always be the same as the thing he's doing in your neighbor. May we have humility when we approach each other, and resist imposing the things God asks of us on other folks. May we trust the Holy Spirit, who convicts of sin and gives wisdom, who still speaks today, and who works in diversity. May we love our neighbors as ourselves. We all need people who will patiently stand by us as we figure some of this stuff out; we need guides not drill sergeants. The beautiful collective of God's people shines most when we come alongside each other and support one another in our God-given assignments, not arrogantly assert they follow God down the same path we're on. Sometimes Christ meets someone on their path while they're a reviled tax collector, or while they're a revered teacher of the Torah. Sometimes he meets us while we're raised in a home with conservative values, sometimes he meets us while we're confronting the reality of our sexual orientation. There are many roads that can lead to Jesus, and we're all traveling slowly.

We are Reading the Bible in a Responsible Way

In order to identify how to read the Bible in a responsible way we have to answer two questions. First: What is the Bible? Now, I used to be able to simply say, "it's the word of God," and leave it at that. While I still believe this, responsibility with Scripture requires we unpack what that means, and respond with grace and humility when we find out there are other valid Christian traditions who are not on the same page about how to define the Bible. The second question is: How do we read it? Now, I'm not even going to begin to be able to answer this question cohesively in the subsection of a chapter, so I'll do my best with the minimal space I'm given here, and I'll end this section with recommendations on content I have consumed that has been helpful to me with answering these questions.

Throughout my journey with Christ the Bible has often been the source of my greatest joy. To this day it is my sacred meeting place with God. It has also been the source of my deepest doubt, at times the place where God seemed nonsensical, unlikely, or outright evil. The way I used to read the Bible did not have any sustainability to it, and for a while I not only lost my love for the Scriptures, but actually grew to resent them. However, as I write this I do so with a greater love and appreciation for the Bible than I ever have. We all have a way of reading the Scriptures, a lens we apply to interpret the text. All Bible reading is interpreted reading. None of us are able to pick up the Scriptures and read it through the lens of the ancient near Eastern audience the Bible was written by and for. Because of our modern contexts, we are all having to apply interpretive measures to draw meaning from the text. As contemporary Westerners, it can be reasonably asserted we are not an oppressed ancient near Eastern people. The way I read the Bible is impacted by the experiences I've had with God, the faith tradition I was brought up in, and the way I exercise reasoning. All of these factors filter my interpretations of the Scripture. I say again, all Scripture reading is interpreted reading. Acknowledging this is paramount in handling the Bible responsibly.

When I talk about the lens we use to interpret Scriptures I do so with the assumption there are several lenses one could apply to extract meaning. Yes, the Bible is inspired, but how is it inspired? Is it only inspired if you

WHAT IS A HEALTHY CONSTRUCT?

take it as literally as possible? Is it still inspired if you believe parts of it are allegory or poetry? I believed, and vehemently taught, a way of reading the Bible that robbed it of human influences all throughout Scripture. I made it to sound like the Scriptures were given to us on gold tablets from heaven. Once I learned about biblical authorship, I had this idea in my head of God putting the authors in a trance so as to make sure it was perfectly penned (as I understand perfection from a postmodern perspective). But what if God penned the Scriptures by partnering with the authors' humanity, not bypassing it? Does the Bible lose its inspiration if you acknowledge God worked with people to pen the Scriptures? People with cultures, limitations, languages, and contexts?

Because of the age of enlightenment in the eighteenth century many of us live with a binary view of the physical and the Divine. Many Christians believe we live in a natural world where the occasional supernatural occurrence will take place. There is the physical and then there's the spiritual, the earthly and the heavenly, and the two are firmly separated. Yet the biblical authors did not have such a binary view of the physical and the spiritual. Where we see separation, they see unity. The whole image of the garden of Eden is a picture of a perfectly unified heaven and earth. Time and time again in the Scriptures, when we see God using people he does not do so at the expense of their humanity but in participation with it. When penning the Scriptures, God didn't work independently from humans but in and through them.

> But what if God penned the Scriptures by partnering with the authors' humanity, not bypassing it? Does the Bible lose its inspiration if you acknowledge God worked with people to pen the Scriptures? People with cultures, limitations, languages, and contexts?

In addition to not having a comprehensive understanding of what the Bible was and how it came to be, I was unaware there were other lenses that could be used to extract meaning from the text. I held a flat reading of Scripture, which is to say the Bible was like Kansas to me. Here's what I mean: a few years ago, Jordan and I made a cross-country road trip from New York to Oregon. My favorite states to drive through were Colorado, Utah, and Wyoming. I loved the large mountains, hills, and curvy roads in the middle of nature. I loved the massive cloudy skies in Wyoming hovering over the mountains, reminding us all of how small we were. It was enough to bring me to tears. Then, we drove through Kansas. Kansas was miles and miles of flat farmland. No dimension, mountains, hills, or big buildings. Just miles of flatness. Now, if you're a fan of Kansas, God bless you and keep you. The hours driving through Kansas were the longest hours of my life.

The way I used to read the Bible reminds me a lot of Kansas. In Kansas, you can see what feels like miles in any direction because it's all flat land. In a similar vein, the way I used to read the Bible held that every piece of the Scriptures was as uniquely authoritative and relevant to my life today as it was in the context it was written, unless elsewhere in the Scriptures relieved me from being bound to certain laws or commands. I take a more nuanced view of the Bible today. I have heard it said that rather than viewing the Bible as a large plot of flat land, we ought to view it as a valley with a hill in the center. On the hill, you get the best view of what everything else in the valley looks like. I have found the Bible to be at its most authoritative, inspired, and relevant for life today when we place the Gospels as the hill in the valley of Scripture. When we stand on the hill of the Gospels we get the best view of what the Bible is saying to us as Christians today. Rather than insisting on a hermeneutic of infallibility, a way of reading the Bible that insists it must be read as a perfect account of science and history (as we understand science and history today), I suggest to approach the Bible as one unified story pointing to Jesus and guiding us along the path of living and believing like Jesus.

Now, there are plenty of reputable biblical scholars who would probably take umbrage with this. People I deeply respect on varying places of the theological spectrum, like Timothy Keller and Peter Enns, take a different reading of the Bible, and I continue to learn invaluable things about life and faith from their work. But for me, I have seen the Bible come alive most with what I've heard called the Christocentric hermeneutic. We all approach the Bible with assumptions, biases, cultural conditioning, and a whole mental encyclopedia we have produced since birth to make sense of the world. As a Christian, as a little Christ, the work of the Spirit in my life is one of forming Christ in me. And if you are a follower of Jesus, the same is true for you. This does not mean we disregard the rest of the Scriptures, or that it is only the Gospels that are truly God-breathed. Rather, we acknowledge all of Scripture points to Jesus, and because of this we read all of Scripture with the supremacy of Christ as our lens.

Please know I am not advocating for a reading of Scripture that is less divine. Tim Mackie pitched this idea in The Bible Project's online classes: the human origins of Scriptures do not negate or diminish its divine word

WHAT IS A HEALTHY CONSTRUCT?

or authority, but its divine word and authority does not diminish the human process that brought them into existence. We undermine its power to speak when we force it into the "golden tablets from heaven" paradigm. Do we consider Jesus less the son of God because he spoke Aramaic, which he learned from his historically located mom and Joseph? There is not a single instance in Scripture where God works with or uses a person by placing them under a spell that relieves them of their autonomy. Why should we believe the penning of the Scriptures is any different? Are we willing to concede God wants to work his will out in the world through humans? The Bible is a uniquely special place where God speaks to his people and points them to Jesus, and it has an ongoing story it is inviting us to participate in.

Below is a list of recommended content for helping to answer the complex questions of what the Bible is and how it can be read responsibly.

Free Internet Stuff/Podcasts:

The Bible Project. Anything and everything by them. I cannot speak higher of their YouTube videos, podcast, and graduate-level online Bible courses. Start here and consume everything you can.

Theology Curator and *The Paulcast* with Kurt Willems.

Theology in the Raw with Preston Sprinkle.

The Bible for Normal People with Peter Enns and Jared Byas.

Exploring My Strange Bible with Dr. Tim Mackie.

Books:

The New Testament in its World by N. T. Wright.

Fight by Preston Sprinkle. Although this is not necessarily a book about biblical hermeneutics, Preston does an excellent job unpacking what a healthy lens for Scripture reading can be.

Inspired Imperfection by Greg Boyd.

The Bible Tells Me So and *How the Bible Actually Works* by Peter Enns.

Inspired by Rachel Held Evans.

What is the Bible? by Rob Bell.

PART II: A FAITH WORTH PASSING DOWN

Blue Parakeet by Scott McKnight.

Theology and the Old Testament by Walter Brueggemann.

We are Revealing What God Looks Like

Ask any random person on the street what God looks like, and you will get a plethora of answers. Ask anyone in the church what God looks like, and you are still likely to get myriad answers. The truth is, as the people of God, we are the chosen vessel God has selected to reveal himself to the world. This was certainly the case for Israel in the Hebrew Bible. The Torah laid out a comprehensive list of what their conduct ought to be in order to reveal God as best they could in their moment of time and space. Over 200 times in the Old Testament the Hebrew word *checed* is used (with the C pronounced like you've got popcorn stuck in your throat). *Checed* in the Bible is God's covenant faithfulness to his people. It is often used to describe God's loving-kindness and goodness. The people of Israel were recipients of Yaweh's *checed*, and were called to pass it along to each other. In doing so they would reveal to the ancient world around them what God looked like.

Today, we have a fuller revelation of what God looked like than even the people of ancient Israel. When we behold Jesus, we see what God looks like. In John 14 Jesus confounds his disciples by telling them they have known and seen the Father. Philip asks Jesus to show them the Father, which seems reasonable. If I had been told I have seen God and thought I missed it, I would be the first to ask for clarity. But how Jesus responds is so important. He says, "I have been with you all this time, Philip, and you still don't know me? Whoever has seen me has seen the Father. How can you say, 'Show us the Father?'" When Moses asked to see the face of God all he could stomach in the moment was to see God's back as he passed Mt. Sinai. But in that moment, the disciples were standing before God face to face. The revelation of God grew before the community discretely and unexpectedly, like a mustard seed. They had not known that all this time they were walking side by side with God, like Adam and Eve had in the garden. I could not hit this point home better than the author of Hebrews if I tried, so I'm not going to.

Hebrews 1:1–3 reads, "Long ago God spoke to our ancestors in many and various ways by the prophets, but in these last days he has spoken to us by a Son, whom he appointed heir of all things, through whom he also

WHAT IS A HEALTHY CONSTRUCT?

created the worlds. He is the reflection of God's glory and the exact imprint of God's very being, and he sustains all things by his powerful word."

It is of ultimate importance that we do not miss this. God's method of communication, or revelation, was through prophets in the time period of the Old Testament. But in these days, he speaks and reveals through his Son. This Son is the reflection of God's glory. Just as when you look in a mirror you see your own reflection, when we look at Christ we see the reflection of God. He is the exact imprint of God's very being. As Brian Zahnd has repeatedly said in his sermons, "God is like Jesus. God has always been like Jesus. There has never been a time in time when God was not like Jesus. We have not always known this, but now we do." This is why the Christocentric hermeneutic we referenced earlier is so important. It doesn't matter how you read the Bible, I don't see there being a way to faithfully read Scripture or view God than through the lens of Jesus.

Why am I hitting this home so much? Why is it so important to boldly and uncomplicatedly say Jesus is the exact representation of God's being? Because the fruit of our lives will always reflect the ideology at our core. I have not always believed Jesus was the definitive revelation of God. I spent years believing Jesus really loved me, and he had to protect me from his angry Father. We do violence to the Trinity when we embrace this as a theological stance. Not only do we do violence to the Trinity, but we do violence to our witness of the gospel. As I stated earlier, as the people of God we are called to reveal God to the world. We are to bear witness to the revelation of Jesus.

If your average non-Christian were to watch Jerry Fallwell Jr. or Franklin Graham do an interview on Fox News or CNN where they angrily raged against folks who disagreed with the comments and behavior of Donald Trump, what would they think God looks like? If you were not a Christian, and you heard Donald Rumsfeld reference the book of Joshua before the US stormed Iraq, implying that just as the Israelites had to conquer the Canaanites so we have to conquer the Middle East, what would you think of God? Or let's go back to my friend Jack from the halfway house, who saw that article on the internet speaking of a preacher who claimed God blessed him with a ten-million-dollar home. My friend Jack, who had begged God to rescue him for years from his torture to no avail, very understandably came to the conclusion God was either cruel, arbitrary, or nonexistent.

You will be hard pressed to see much of the image of Jesus in any of the previously listed examples. It's easy to throw stones at people in places of influence and the public arena. And while part of me agrees that if you're going to have such a public platform you subject yourself to public scrutiny, I know that too much of this "calling out" only serves to distract from the ways in which I myself have not represented the image of Christ to the world. I have helped the church paint an un-Christlike picture of God, and I'll say it again, most people aren't leaving churches in droves because they have a problem with Jesus. We pastors strategize, cast visions, implement new programs, attend conferences, read books, and host team meetings to try and plug the hole that's leaking people, and I affirm and love all of those things, but we are wasting our time if we are not starting with the most important question of all: Does the way we do church represent Christ to the world? Does our preaching reflect the inclusive, come-and-see attitude of Jesus? Does the way we steward our finances reflect the radical generosity Jesus expected of his followers? Does the way we foster community reflect the gracious, come-as-you-are, service-oriented, enemy-loving, justice-concerned ethic of Jesus? All the programs and vision casting in the world won't solve the church's deepest problems until we address these things first.

As Christians, our primary task is to reveal who God is to the world. And the good news is God is like Jesus. We do this so much better when we embody it than when we pontificate about it. As I write this, communities all over the world have been devastated by the outbreak of COVID-19. Friends have lost their jobs, hours are being cut, the economy is tanking, anxiety is on the rise, and fear is the new normal. And I have seen churches step up above and beyond to meet the needs of their community. One church is dipping into their savings to pay bills for out-of-work congregants. Another one is rallying together to purchase gift cards to grocery stores for anyone in need. Staff members are going out of their way to call every person in their church directories to talk for hours with folks who are scared, isolated, and hopeless. People are being noticed in this season in a way they would not have been on an average Sunday morning. I have a lot of hope for the church. We have a way of surpassing expectations and rising to the occasion. When we let him, Jesus will always lead his church, and we can spot whether or not we are being led by Jesus based on whether or not our community embodies his life.

CHAPTER THIRTEEN

Regenerate

"People who've had any genuine spiritual experience always know that they don't know. They are utterly humbled before mystery. They are in awe before the abyss of it all, in wonder at eternity and depth, and a Love, which is incomprehensible to the mind."
—RICHARD ROHR

"Remain in me, and I will remain in you."
—JOHN 15:4 (NIV)

Literally Scared for Our Lives

MY WIFE AND I decided to go on one last date as an affianced couple the month before we got married. We wanted to do something a little special to get away from the hustle of wedding planning. I was working four jobs at the time. You read that right: four jobs. I was working eighty hours a week, sleeping three hours a night, and pretending to help plan a wedding. Kelsey and I had not gotten any quality time in what felt like months. So, we decided to take a small road trip to Sisters, Oregon.

The trip from our city of Springfield, Oregon to Sisters is about two hours. We would get plenty of time to connect on the car ride there and back, eat at a touristy restaurant, and drink coffee at my favorite coffee roasters in the world (shout out to Sisters Coffee Company). It was a great

PART II: A FAITH WORTH PASSING DOWN

date, and the drive up out of the Willamette Valley was relatively snow-free considering it was mid-November.

After our day in Sisters we headed home. Now, if you have ever driven from Sisters to Springfield you know there are two routes you can take. There is the quick way, and then there is the scenic route. We were not in a hurry to get back to the chaos of home, so we opted for the scenic route. We traveled up the road, and the more we drove, the snowier it got. The roads slimmed down to the point where our one-way lane became a two-way lane without changing sizes.

As the snow picked up and the roads grew windier, I slowed down significantly. While driving slowly up a frozen mountain my wife and I were disturbed to see a furious-looking man walking toward us on the side of the road. The man wore a bright orange sweater and a baseball cap. What was this guy doing alone all the way up here in a snowstorm? He walked from one side of the road to the other where he would be on Kelsey's side of the car as we drove past him. I attempted to speed past him but the tires slipped and spun, refusing to permit us any additional speed. We slowly drove by the mysterious man as he scowled at us from the side of the road, glaring the entire time.

We drove on, both deeply unsettled. It was close to an hour before the snow on the road got so thick my 2005 Chevy Cobalt was never going to make it. I got out and dug the snow out from under the tires to give us enough space to attempt to turn around. I asked my wife to stay in the car, partially to be chivalrous, mostly because I could see she was so unsettled by the man earlier that getting out of the car would have been too much. I did not have the proper tools, gloves, or even a jacket. The snow fell hard as I finished digging around the tires. I got in my car and attempted to maneuver our way in the opposite direction. I got us turned around, but the car got stuck again. As I was struggling, my soon-to-be-wife screamed loud enough you would have thought she saw a ghost. It was not a ghost, but it wasn't much more comforting. Looking ahead down the dark road, thanks to my high-beams, we were barely able to make out the image of the scowling man as he walked toward us.

Thoughts raced through my mind as panic started to set in. *Did he turn around to follow us? He must have known how snowy it was up here, he must have known my car was never going to make it.* I reasoned he was either approaching to help us or hurt us, and I did not want to stick around to find out which it was. I threw the car into drive and slammed on the gas. The car slipped and spun before catching traction and began zooming down the road. I prayed the man would step out of the way, and he did, glaring at us as we passed him.

We returned home, safe and sound. My wife and I enjoy telling the story now, but in the moment we were terrified.

A Predictable Path

I learned a valuable lesson about the importance of properly preparing for your road trips that evening. Without checking weather conditions, properly chaining my tires, consulting a map, or even wearing appropriate clothes, Kelsey and I found ourselves in a potentially dangerous situation. The path we were on could have been predicted had we taken the proper precautions. Somebody with more experience and, well, common sense than myself could have told you something like that would have happened. In his book, *The Principle of the Path*, Andy Stanley tells us "Direction, not intention, leads us to our destination." My intentions were good, I wanted to spend more time with my fiancé before returning to the chaotic life waiting for us back home, but the path I was on did not lead us to a good destination. Direction, not intention, leads us to our destination.

For as long as I can remember, churches have been ringing the gong to let people know my generation and generations after me were going to be leaving in droves. They rang this gong as the generation before me started their mass exodus. And now, the American Christian church's witness to the world is complicated at best, but mostly tarnished. Now, unfair representation in media has not helped. And I'm not even talking about mainstream media. Sure, Amanda Bynes's character in the movie *Easy A* did not make Christians look good, but none of the Christians in *God's Not Dead* spoke of something beautiful to the world. Influence of media aside, the church has been traveling down a path, leaving a wake of disenchanted people behind her, for a long time, and the outcome could have been prevented.

For all the wonderful and beautiful things churches have presented to the world in the last seventy years, we have also taken up an ugly yoke. Whether it is pastors buying multi-million-dollar homes and private jets, televangelists manipulating people into funding their "nonprofit" operations, Christians tirelessly seeking to legislate the morality of the world around them, their blatant homophobia, racism, and sexism, or the sexual assault, financial scandals, and shameful theology being preached from the pulpit, something in the recent sordid history of the American church could have tipped us off to the fact that this mass exodus was coming.

It came. It's here. But the Christian movement is far from over. If the path we were headed down could have been predicted, then it stands to reason we can adjust our course properly, and predict where we are headed from here. The church has always thrived on the margins. We have to move forward, and here's where I think some helpful starting places might be.

1. Give People Permission to Wrestle

We must give people explicit permission to wrestle through this stuff. These things are not always easy to believe, and there is no shortage of spiritual alternatives being offered by the rest of the world. We must surrender our fear and suspicion of the doubting ones—they are seeing things we need pointed out to us. I once heard a pastor say every church needs to provide a space where people are given permission to voice their doubts, and where they are allowed to be heretics without fear of being corrected.

> You are free to doubt. You are free to question. You are free to wrestle with the Divine. We are a people built on that struggle. And when we shed the lie that keeps us suffering and doubting in silence, and we enter into this Divine struggle, there is blessing.

Jacob wrestled God, and came out on the other side blessed with a new name, and a revelation of his true self. The name Israel in Hebrew, like so much in the Hebrew language, is much less a word than it is a symbol. The word gives the picture of one who wrestles with the Divine and is blessed. When God gave this name to Jacob, and eventually an entire nation, they became a nation of people marked by a struggle with the Divine, and by their discovery of blessing and new identity. The Christian tradition I ascribe to is one of wrestling with God. It's a tradition with a Bible of people on record saying:

"My people have been slaughtered."

"My temple has been destroyed"

"My family has been taken off to Babylon."

"My God, my God, why have you forsaken me?"

Loss. Fear. Doubt. What does anything mean when it feels your ground of being is stripped away? This wrestling with God is a major crux in the Christian (and Jewish) faith. We neuter our tradition when we rob it of this pivotal dialogue about the nature and existence of God. You are free to doubt. You are free to question. You are free to wrestle with the Divine. We are a people built on that struggle. And when we shed the lie that keeps us suffering and doubting in silence, and we enter into this Divine struggle, there is blessing. Our true selves lie on the other side of the struggle. The people who have wrestled with God, they walk with a limp, but they have experienced the Divine. We are in the spiritual lineage of the people of Israel. The people who struggle with the Divine come out blessed on the other side.

2. Let Go

I said earlier that deconstruction is a terrible and a beautiful trend. Beautiful because some things in our tradition need to be seriously reconsidered. In this cultural moment, the church is being afforded an opportunity of genuine rebirth. Churches all over the world are taking the steps to repent and more beautifully present Christ to the world. In my state alone, one church has moved heaven and earth to offer a higher level of inclusion to folks who have felt the sting of rejection from their religious communities. Another church has tirelessly worked to honor the biblical mandate to care for the widows and orphans, members of this church house the majority of the foster kids in their city. My friend Bill MacDonald and late pastor/boss/spiritual father Dave Lanning dreamed of adopting the most aggressively turbulent middle school in our city. Our church has provided money, meals, school supplies, gifts, and clothes to families in this school. When Dave launched the vision for this, he instructed the church that they were not to preach at anyone while doing this, to let the church's actions speak for the gospel.

More and more churches are rising to the occasion of justice and healing. And if this trend is to continue, we must disentangle our deep ties to American idealism, consumerism, power-mongering, greed, and injustice. The world has no tolerance for it anymore, nor should it. In 2006, The Episcopal Church released a guide on global poverty titled *God's Mission in the World*. In it, Desmond Tutu says, "I don't preach a social gospel; I preach the Gospel. Period. The gospel of our Lord Jesus Christ is concerned with the whole person. When people were hungry, Jesus didn't say 'Now, is that political or social?' He said, 'I feed you.' Because the good news to a hungry person is bread."

In Luke 4, we see Jesus entering the temple. He stands before a crowd and opens a scroll that contains the words from the poet/prophet Isaiah. Verses 18–19 of this book reveal what the scroll said, "The Spirit of God is upon me, for he has anointed me to bring the good news to the poor. He has sent me to proclaim that the captives will be released, the blind will see, that the oppressed will be set free, and that the time of the Lord's favor has come."

This was the gospel message Jesus preached to announce the beginning of his ministry. The church is called to embody the reality of this proclamation, and I believe many churches are headed there. But we still have much that needs to be surrendered. So, may we be brave in our letting go.

3. Hold on

Dear faithful skeptic,

Above all else, hang on to Jesus, the precious center of our faith. The world around you will fail you, religious institutions will fail you, theology will fail you, church members and leaders will inevitably fail you, but Jesus will not. He is the good news your soul is searching for. He is the *shalom* our world needs. I don't know what journey has led you to this book. I don't know what pains, betrayals, doubts, rejections, and traumas you have endured on your journey, but I believe if you have made it this far into the book there is still something in you humming for the reality of Christ. It is okay to doubt, it is okay to be angry, it is okay to question how it is possible for you to have faith when the faithful have contributed to so much ugliness in the world. It's okay to embrace the tension of experience and doctrine, where what you see and feel is not lining up with what you have been told is true. You are on a blessed journey. I want to urge you to hold on to Jesus, but if you need to let go, if you need space, that is okay. You are still of immeasurable value. And know this: even if you to let God go, God won't let you go. God is all around you. If you look long enough, you'll see him. Hang in there. I promise, it's worth it.

God is with you.

Dear faithful friend of skeptics,

Thank you for the stability you bring into the world of us faithful skeptics. Undoubtedly by now you have seen loved ones suffer through a crisis of faith. Pray for them. Embrace them. Love them. Hang on to them. There may be a season where faith is not an option for them, where they let go of everything they knew and loved, and if that season comes, they need you to hang on to them. Be a nonanxious presence in their lives. The best thing you can do for somebody who tells you they don't believe anymore is offer a hug; not a Bible verse, not fear, not interrogation—a hug. As they are letting go, hold on to them. Don't let them go. Allow your faith to hold space for the doubt they are experiencing. You have what it takes.

God is with you.

Regenerate

Many great spiritual leaders and teachers today are insisting it is not enough to merely deconstruct, that some form of reconstruction must follow. It isn't enough to take something apart, you have to put it back together. May our faith not merely be put back together, but may it be done so with complete moral reform. May we regenerate our faith so we may revive anew and bring into existence a tradition that is beneficial to the world. The church will always have critics, especially as America enters into an era where ideology is more formed by facetious memes than it is by experience and interpersonal relationships. There will always be someone mocking and sneering at people of faith. For most of my life people have pointed to Christians as proof for why there can't be a God. How can we expect people to believe when the faithful are so unbelievable? May we regenerate the way of Jesus, a way so full of peace, charity, and grace that even those who would never intellectually concede to believe in a God might say, "I want to say I don't believe in God, but then how do you explain Christians?" May the way of our being mirror the truths we hold dearly. May our conduct reflect the goodness of God, not turn people away from it.

God is on the move. He is looking for co-laborers and partners. He is the stream that is following in the direction of healing and restoration. My hope, dear reader, is not that you would merely deconstruct and reconstruct, but that your faith would be regenerated, more vibrant and beautiful than before. A friend of mine once pointed out to me that when people and communities experience intense pain and stress it is a sign that either a breakthrough or a breakdown is on the way. We have seen the church in breakdown mode for a long time, but I have a sense we are approaching a time for breakthrough, a time to regenerate.

Acknowledgments

Thank you . . .

Kelsey Scarcello: for your constant love and support. For the light, joy, wholeness, courage, and stability you bring to my world. You are more the girl of my dreams today than eight years ago. You brave my big emotions, hold space for my doubt, and have consistently incarnated God's love for me more than I could ever earn.

Matthew Wimer: for coming up with the idea to put my story to paper, being my editor, believing in me, advocating for me to the publishing company, encouraging me to persevere when I wanted to quit, and for being one of my best friends. This book would not exist without you. There are no words to describe the gratitude I feel for having your wisdom and friendship in my life.

Dad: for staying when many fathers would have left for much less. Thank you for modeling loyalty, strength, protection, courage, endurance, work ethic, and love. Thank you for unannounced visits, and always finding ways to care for the people around you. You're my best friend, and I love you.

Jordan Magill and Dennis MacFarland: for being my family when my own family was falling apart. For sharing with me every horrible event, joyful moment, and everything in between since I was sixteen. There is no version of who I am today without you two. You challenge me, inspire me, encourage me, and have never given up on me. Most people don't get friends like you. I am fortunate beyond measure to be a recipient of your love.

Brennan Scarcello: for modeling a fighting spirit, for hanging on to your smarts and tenderness through unspeakable pain. You are my hero.

PART II: A FAITH WORTH PASSING DOWN

Blancher Family: Paul, you are my pastor, mentor, second father, a personal hero, and one of my closest friends. Carole, because of you I am not a motherless son; words fail to tell of how much I love you. Lainey, you are the great improver in my life, my sister, and one of my dearest friends. Thank God for your passionate conviction and strong moral compass.

Grace Wimer: you are my sister in the faith, a person whose wisdom and insight I rely on, and one of the funnest people in my world.

Daniel Lanning: I considered your dad a father in the faith so it is only natural to consider you a big brother in the faith. Thank you for reading early drafts and providing much-needed insight. Being your friend and working by your side has been the best motivation I could have to up my game as a pastor, because to work with you is to work with one of the best pastors I've ever known.

Steve Erickson: even when I was not sure I believed in God anymore, you prophesied that I would be back to work as a pastor. You are, beyond a shadow of a doubt, the best pastor I know. I don't know what I did to deserve a father in the faith like you.

Kurt Willems: for being a coach, mentor, friend, spiritual director, and deeply trusted pastoral voice in my life. Your wisdom and kindness are blessings to me. For reading the project early on and providing feedback.

Kevin Lemieux: for being the best counselor I could fathom. You offer the best input, drink great scotch, and read the good stuff. It is like God made you in a machine for me.

Jeremy Carlton: for knowing the words that bring life, and using your gift of articulation and intensity to raise courage in me. Your unwavering support and belief in me have been more formative than you could know. Thank you for reading early drafts and providing impeccable insight.

Ryan Cole: for your encouragement, brotherhood, teachability (which reminds me to do the same), and for bringing much-needed joy into my life.

A. J. Swoboda: your faith in me, my calling, and this project has provided much-needed affirmation as I embark on this journey. Thank you for letting me bounce ideas off you, but more importantly, for modeling wholehearted discipleship. I'm just following you on the trail you blaze.

Preston Sprinkle: there is not enough space in the book to properly unpack how pivotal of a role you have played in my life. Thank you for being my theology answer man, for your friendship, guidance, and courage.

Tim Johnson: you are a rescuer. You rescue people who are falling so fast into the mystery it feels like they won't survive the landing. Without God seeing fit to introduce me to you, I would not be writing a book full of hope for the church.

David Krantz: for consistent friendship, being an over-the-top joy of a roommate to Kels and I, and giving me space to laugh or scream.

Christian Brown: for believing in the project early on, for reading early drafts and providing insight, for teaching me about the creative process, and for loving Switchfoot as much as I do.

Alec Crisman: the list of people in my life more encouraging, thoughtful, or challenging in all the right ways is short. You've been that for me since freshman year of high school, and I will always rely on your voice.

Andrew Beaird: for being my first mentor, spiritual teacher, occasional theological sparring partner, and a lifelong friend.

Lindsey and Tyler Robinson: when I thought my hopes and dreams were dashed for good, your house with your family was the space I went to find hope. Your love has been church to Kelsey and I.

Brandon Loescher: for being a prophetic voice in my life, and refusing to let me settle for less than full-blown kingdom living.

Stacy Swartout-McKee: when I was a high school kid whose world was falling apart, you let me cry in your office between classes. You gave me hope, and defined reality. What you have done for me, and so many other students at Springfield High School, can never be repaid.

Chris Plumb: for being the first person to coach me in my writing, and telling me I had potential. If this book sucks, I blame you.

Springfield Faith Center Church: for being a hotbed of warmth, generosity, and love, and for teaching me how to be a pastor again.

Bibliography

Bates, Matthew. *Salvation by Allegiance Alone*. Ada, MI: Baker Academic, 2017.
Bethke, Jefferson. *It's Not What You Think*. Nashville: Thomas Nelson, 2015.
The Bible Project. "The Way of the Exile." https://www.youtube.com/watch?v=XzWpaogcPyo.
Brown, Brene. *The Gifts of Imperfection*. Center City, MN: Hazelden, 2010.
Claiborne, Shane. *The Irresistible Revolution*. Grand Rapids: Zondervan, 2006.
Dawkins, Richard. *The God Delusion*. 2006. Reprint edition. Boston: Mariner, 2008.
Derrida, Jacques. *Of Grammatology*. Fortieth Anniversary edition. Baltimore: Johns Hopkins University Press, 2016.
Fischer, Austin. *Young, Restless, and No Longer Reformed*. Eugene, OR: Cascade, 2014.
Ham, Ken. *Already Gone*. New York: Master, 2009.
Lamott, Anne. *Plan B*. New York: Riverhead, 2005.
Marx, Karl. *Critique of Hegel's "Philosophy of Right."* Cambridge: Cambridge University Press, 2009.
Murray, Stuart. *The Naked Anabaptist*. Herald; Fifth Anniversary Edition, 2015.
Niequest, Aaron. *The Eternal Current*. Colorado Springs: WaterBrook, 2018.
Pew Research Center. "America's Changing Religious Landscape." https://www.pewforum.org/2015/05/12/americas-changing-religious-landscape/
Ricoeur, Paul. *The Symbolism of Evil*. Boston: Beacon, 1986.
Rohr, Richard. *The Naked Now*. Chestnut Ridge, NY: Crossroad, 2009.
Sprinkle, Preston. *Fight*. Colorado Springs: David C. Cook, 2013.
———. *People to be Loved*. Grand Rapids: Zondervan, 2015.
Sproul, R. C. "Why Did God Command the Children of Israel to Kill Every Man, Woman, and Child in the Promised Land?" https://www.ligonier.org/search/?q=killing&teachers=R.C. percent20Sproul
Stanley, Andy. *The Principle of the Path*. Nashville: Thomas Nelson, 2011.
Swoboda, A. J. *The Dusty Ones*. Ada, MI: Baker, 2016.
———. *Subversive Sabbath*. Ada, MI: Brazos, 2018.
Tutu, Desmond. https://episcopalchurch.org/posts/publicaffairs/episcopal-presiding-bishop-archbishop-desmond-tutu-discuss-mission-live-webcast
Wright, N. T. *Surprised by Hope*. San Francisco: HarperOne, 2008.
Zahnd, Brian. *Water to Wine: Some of My Story*. Middleton, ID: Spello, 2016.

www.ingramcontent.com/pod-product-compliance
Lightning Source LLC
Chambersburg PA
CBHW051107160426
43193CB00010B/1344